Basic English Grammar for Kids

5

JN073965

Section 1 | Grammar 1~4 Review 1 | Alphabet & Vowels

Write the uppercase and the lowercase letters.
（大文字と小文字を書こう！）

Uppercase（大文字） ⟶

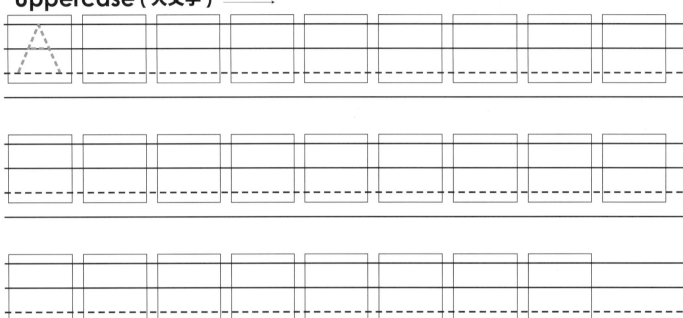

Lowercase（小文字） ⟶

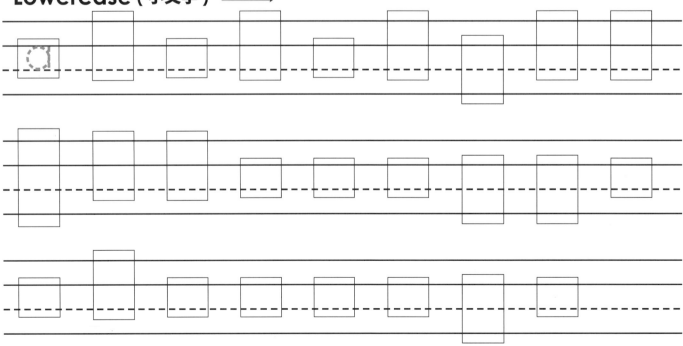

 Circle the vowels below.
（母音をみつけて全部に ◯ をつけよう！）

cucumber

pumpkin

tomato

onion

cabbage

carrot

potato

lettuce

green pepper

spinach

bean

corn

broccoli

Review! Write the vowels.（母音を書こう！）

Uppercase（大文字）				

Lowercase（小文字）				

Write "a" or "an" on the lines. (▭ に "a" か "an" を書こう！)

① It is _____ elephant.

② It is _____ peach.

③ It is _____ x-ray.

④ It is _____ orange.

⑤ It is _____ clock.

⑥ It is _____ uniform.

特別なルール ☞ 世界に1つだけしかないものは数えなくてもいいよね。

だから、"a" や "an" は使わない。そのかわり "the" を使うよ！

 It is ~~a~~ sun. ➡ It is **the** sun.

It is ~~a~~ moon. ➡ It is **the** moon.

It is ~~an~~ Earth. ➡ It is **the** Earth.

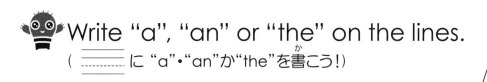 Write "a", "an" or "the" on the lines.
(_____ に "a"・"an"か"the"を書こう！)

ヒント！
どんな時に
"an"や"the"を
使うのかな？

① It is _____ alligator.

② It is _____ moon.

③ It is _____ chair.

④ It is _____ eggplant.

⑤ It is _____ ruler.

⑥ It is _____ sun.

⑦ It is _____ notebook.

⑧ It is _____ Earth.

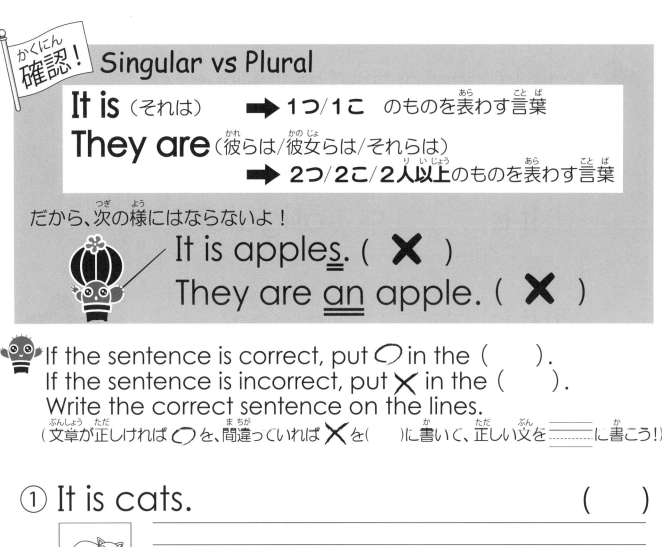

It is (それは) ➡ 1つ/1こ のものを表わす言葉

They are (彼らは/彼女らは/それらは)
➡ 2つ/2こ/2人以上のものを表わす言葉

だから、次の様にはならないよ！

It is apple<u>s</u>. (✖)
They are <u>an</u> apple. (✖)

If the sentence is correct, put ⭕ in the ( ).
If the sentence is incorrect, put ✖ in the ( ).
Write the correct sentence on the lines.
(文章が正しければ ⭕ を、間違っていれば ✖ を( )に書いて、正しい文を ═══ に書こう！)

① It is cats. ( )

② They are a cow. ( )

③ It is a mouse. ( )

④ They are an apron. ( )

⑤ They are glasses. ( )

Rearrange the words to make a sentence.

(( )内の言葉を並べかえて ＿＿＿ に正しい文を作ろう！)

文のはじめの文字は 大文字になるよ！

① (is / it / . / acorn / an)

② (trees / are / . / they)

③ (they / . / grapes / are)

④ (it / sun / the / . / is)

⑤ (are / they / pants / .)

⑥ (mouse / . / it / a / is)

⑦ (an / ostrich / is / . / it)

⑧ (it / the / moon / is / .)

Choose the correct word and write it on the lines.

（正しい言葉を下から選んで ======== の上に書こう！）

① They are _____ .

② It is a _____ .

③ They are _____ .

④ It is an _____ .

⑤ They are _____ .

⑥ It is a _____ .

⑦ They are _____ .

⑧ It is a _____ .

gloves / glove / potatoes / potato
onions / onion / socks / sock

Write "It is" or "They are" on the lines.
（＿＿＿＿ に " It is " か " They are " を書^かこう!）

① _____ glasses.

② _____ an oven.

③ _____ pants.

④ _____ a plate.

⑤ _____ the moon.

⑥ _____ an umbrella.

⑦ _____ the sun.

⑧ _____ shoes.

注　メガネはレンズが2枚^{まい}だね！
ズボンは足^{あし}が2本^{ほんはい}入るよ！
⇒　だから「They are 〜s.」になる。
靴^{くつ}は1つの時^{とき}には「shoe」と言^いうよ、覚^{おぼ}えておこうね!!

Write the Japanese in the (　).
(次の言葉の意味を(　)に日本語で書こう!)

I （　　　　　　）　　We （　　　　　　）

You（　　　　　　）　　You （　　　　　　）

He （　　　　　　）　　They（　　　　　　）

She（　　　　　　）

It （　　　　　　）

Connect the pronouns and *be* verbs below.
(代名詞とbe動詞の am / is / are を線で結ぼう!)

I •

You •

He •　　　　　　　　　　　• am

She •

It •　　　　　　　　　　　• is

We •

You •　　　　　　　　　　　• are

They •

-10-

Write the missing words on the lines.
（_____に英語を書いて文を完成させよう!）

① _____ _____ a German sausage.

（それはドイツソーセージです。）

② _____ _____ Canadian students.

（わたしたちはカナダ人学生です。）

③ _____ _____ Indian students.

（あなたたちはインド人学生です。）

④ _____ _____ British students.

（かれらはイギリス人学生です。）

⑤ _____ _____ a Japanese student.

（わたしは日本人学生です。）

⑥ _____ _____ an American student.

（あなたはアメリカ人学生です。）

⑦ _____ _____ a Chinese student.

（かれは中国人学生です。）

⑧ _____ _____ a Korean student.

（かのじょは韓国人学生です。）

文のはじめの文字は
大文字になるよ!

Write the sentences on the lines.
(_____ に英文を書こう!)

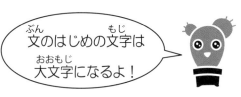
文のはじめの文字は
大文字になるよ!

① わたしは先生です。 (a teacher)

----

② あなたは女優です。 (an actress)

----

③ 彼はパイロットです。 (a pilot)

----

④ 彼女は医者です。 (a doctor)

----

⑤ わたし達は友だちです。 (friends)

----

⑥ それはねずみです。 (a mouse)

----

⑦ 彼らは芸術家です。 (artists)

----

⑧ 彼女たちは先生です。 (teachers)

下のように物(もの)のようすを表わす言葉(ことば)(形容詞(けいようし))がくることもあるよ！

例(れい) **I am tall.** （ぼくは背が高い(せ たか)）

They are young. （かれらは若い(わか)）

この時(とき)は I am ~~a~~ tall. や They are young~~s~~. にはならない！

"tall"や"young"は物(もの)ではないから数えられ(かぞ)ないよ。気(き)をつけてね!!

🤖 Write the sentences on the lines.
(＿＿＿ に英文(えいぶん)を書こう(か)!)

💬 文のはじめ(ぶん)(もじ)の文字は大文字(おおもじ)になるよ！

① わたしはうれしいです。   (happy)

- -

② 彼ら(かれ)はおなかが空いて(す)います。   (hungry)

- -

③ 私たち(わたし)は背が高い(せ)(たか)です。   (tall)

- -

④ 彼(かれ)はおこっています。   (angry)

- -

⑤ あなた達(たち)はかなしいです。   (sad)

- -

⑥ 彼女(かのじょ)はきれいです。   (beautiful)

- -

否定を表わす文を作ろう *Be* Verb + not （〜ではありません）

ルール Be動詞を使った否定の文を作ってみよう！

am / is / are ➕ not ➡ 〜ではありません

ルール Be動詞を使った否定の文は下の順で作るんだよ！

① だれが ➡ ② am is are ➡ ③ not ➡ ④ なに どんな様子 ➡ ⑤ ピリオド （文の終わりの 大切な記号）

【例】 I am **not** a teacher.
（わたしは先生では**ありません**。）

否定（〜ではありません）の文の つくり方は、ここで覚えよう！

Let's read the sentences below. （次の文を読んでみよう！）

check

① I am **not** a nurse.

② You are **not** a doctor.

③ He is **not** a pilot.

④ She is **not** a teacher.

⑤ It is **not** a tree.

⑥ We are **not** police officers.

⑦ You are **not** dentists.

⑧ They are **not** students.

1つに合体できる！ is not ➡ isn't / are not ➡ aren't と、くっつけちゃう時もあるよ！

Rearrange the words to make a sentence.

（（　）内の言葉を並べかえて ＿＿＿ に正しい文を作ろう！）

文のはじめの文字は大文字になるよ！

① わたしは先生ではありません。
(I / a / teacher / not / am / .)

② あなたは女優ではありません。
(an / you / not / . / actress / are)

③ 彼はパイロットではありません。
(is / not / he / . / pilot / a)

④ 彼女は医者ではありません。
(a / she / not / is / doctor / .)

⑤ わたし達は友だちではありません。
(friends / . / not / are / we)

⑥ それはねずみではありません。
(it / not / is / a / mouse / .)

⑦ 彼らは芸術家ではありません。
(artists / they / not / . / are)

Write the sentences on the lines.

（ ------- に英文を書こう!）

① _____ _____ _____ a German sausage.

（それはドイツソーセージではありません。）

② _____ _____ _____ Canadian students.

（わたしたちはカナダ人学生ではありません。）

③ _____ _____ _____ Indian students.

（あなたたちはインド人学生ではありません。）

④ _____ _____ _____ British students.

（かれらはイギリス人学生ではありません。）

⑤ _____ _____ _____ a Japanese student.

（わたしは日本人学生ではありません。）

⑥ _____ _____ _____ an American student.

（あなたはアメリカ人学生ではありません。）

⑦ _____ _____ _____ a Chinese student.

（かれは中国人学生ではありません。）

⑧ _____ _____ _____ a Korean student.

（かのじょは韓国人学生ではありません。）

文のはじめの文字は
大文字になるよ！

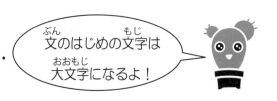

Write the sentences on the lines.

（＿＿＿＿に英文を書こう！）

文のはじめの文字は
大文字になるよ！

① あなたは看護士ではありません。　　　　　　　　(a nurse)

You are ☐ a nurse.

② それはトマトではありません。　　　　　　　　　(a tomato)

It ☐ ☐ a tomato.

③ 彼らは作家ではありません。　　　　　　　　　　(writers)

☐ ☐ ☐ writers.

④ 彼女は図書の先生ではありません。　　　　　　　(a librarian)

☐ ☐ ☐ a librarian.

⑤ 彼は銀行員ではありません。　　　　　　　　　　(a banker)

☐ ☐ ☐ a banker.

⑥ それらはカバではありません。　　　　　　　　　(hippos)

☐ ☐ ☐ hippos.

⑦ 彼女たちは先生ではありません。　　　　　　　　(teachers)

☐ ☐ ☐ teachers.

確認！

You are a boy. ➡ Are you a boy?

だいめいし どうし ばしょ こうかん しつもん ぶん
"代名詞"と"be動詞"は、場所を交換すると質問する文になるんだね！

Write the sentences on the lines.
えいぶん か
(_____に英文を書こう!)

ぶん もじ
文のはじめの文字は
おおもじ
大文字になるよ！

① あなたは看護士ですか？ (a nurse)

② それはトマトですか？ (a tomato)

③ 彼らは作家ですか？ (writers)

④ 彼女は図書の先生ですか？ (a librarian)

⑤ 彼は銀行員ですか？ (a banker)

⑥ それらはカバですか？ (hippos)

Write the sentences on the lines.
(........... に英文を書こう！)

文のはじめの文字は
大文字になるよ！

① あなたは疲れていますか？　　　　　　　　　(tired)

- -

② 彼はねむいですか？　　　　　　　　　　　(sleepy)

- -

③ それは古いですか？　　　　　　　　　　　　(old)

- -

④ 彼らは背が低いですか？　　　　　　　　　(short)

- -

⑤ 彼女はおなかがいっぱいですか？　　　　　　(full)

- -

⑥ あなた達は寒いですか？　　　　　　　　　(cold)

- -

⑦ それらは新しいですか？　　　　　　　　　(new)

- -

⑧ わたし達は速いですか？　　　　　　　　　(fast)

- -

ルール　答える時は次のようにしてね！

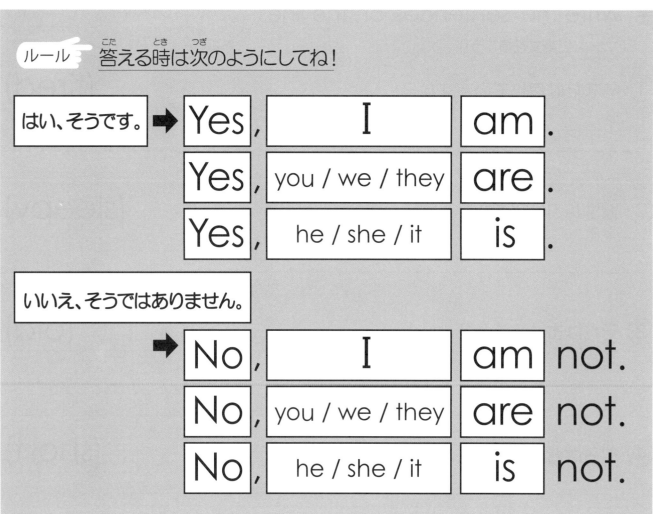

はい、そうです。	➡	Yes,	I	am .
		Yes,	you / we / they	are .
		Yes,	he / she / it	is .

| いいえ、そうではありません。 |
➡ No,	I	am not.
No,	you / we / they	are not.
No,	he / she / it	is not.

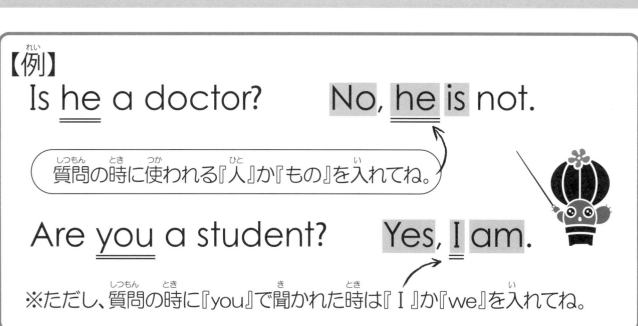

【例】

Is he a doctor?　　　No, he is not.

質問の時に使われる『人』か『もの』を入れてね。

Are you a student?　　Yes, I am.

※ただし、質問の時に『you』で聞かれた時は『I』か『we』を入れてね。

① _____ you a scientist?

Yes, _____ _____ .

② _____ he a pianist?

No, _____ _____ not.

③ _____ she happy?

No, _____ _____ not.

④ _____ it dirty?

Yes, _____ _____ .

⑤ _____ we rich?

_____, _____ _____ .

⑥ _____ they grasshoppers?

_____, _____ _____ _____ .

Choose the correct word from the ▨ and write it on the lines. （絵を見て、それが「どんな」動作か ▨ から選び線の上に書いてみよう！）

りょうり
料理する

_____
- - - - - - - - - - - - - - -
_____

き
切る

_____
- - - - - - - - - - - - - - -
_____

お
押す

_____
- - - - - - - - - - - - - - -
_____

の
飲む

_____
- - - - - - - - - - - - - - -
_____

と
捕る

_____
- - - - - - - - - - - - - - -
_____

た
食べる

_____
- - - - - - - - - - - - - - -
_____

はし
走る

_____
- - - - - - - - - - - - - - -
_____

ある
歩く

_____
- - - - - - - - - - - - - - -
_____

ひら
開く

_____
- - - - - - - - - - - - - - -
_____

ひ
引く

_____
- - - - - - - - - - - - - - -
_____

し
閉める

_____
- - - - - - - - - - - - - - -
_____

い
行く

_____
- - - - - - - - - - - - - - -
_____

catch / open / cook / pull
close / run / eat / drink
walk / push / cut / go

Choose the correct word from the ▮ and write it on the lines. （絵を見て、それが「どんな」動作か ▮ から選び線の上に書いてみよう！）

すわ
座る

_____

- - - - - - - - - - - - - - - -

_____

つ
摘む

_____

- - - - - - - - - - - - - - - -

_____

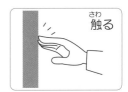
さわ
触る

_____

- - - - - - - - - - - - - - - -

_____

うた
歌う

_____

- - - - - - - - - - - - - - - -

_____

のぼ
登る

_____

- - - - - - - - - - - - - - - -

_____

す
好き

_____

- - - - - - - - - - - - - - - -

_____

よ
読む

_____

- - - - - - - - - - - - - - - -

_____

う
売る

_____

- - - - - - - - - - - - - - - -

_____

つく
作る

_____

- - - - - - - - - - - - - - - -

_____

み
見る

_____

- - - - - - - - - - - - - - - -

_____

と あ
跳び上がる

_____

- - - - - - - - - - - - - - - -

_____

お
置く

_____

- - - - - - - - - - - - - - - -

_____

climb / jump / sit / like

make / look / pick / put

sing / sell / touch / read

Choose the correct word from the ▨ and write it on the lines. （絵を見て、それが「どんな」動作か ▨ から選び線の上に書いてみよう！）

弾く

持っている

書く

寝る

聞く

泳ぐ

描く

移動する

投げる

乗る

飛ぶ

勉強する

sleep / swim / move / throw

have / draw / listen / play

study / write / fly / ride

Choose the correct word from the ▮ and write it on the lines.（絵を見て、それが「どんな」動作か ▮ から選び線の上に書いてみよう！）

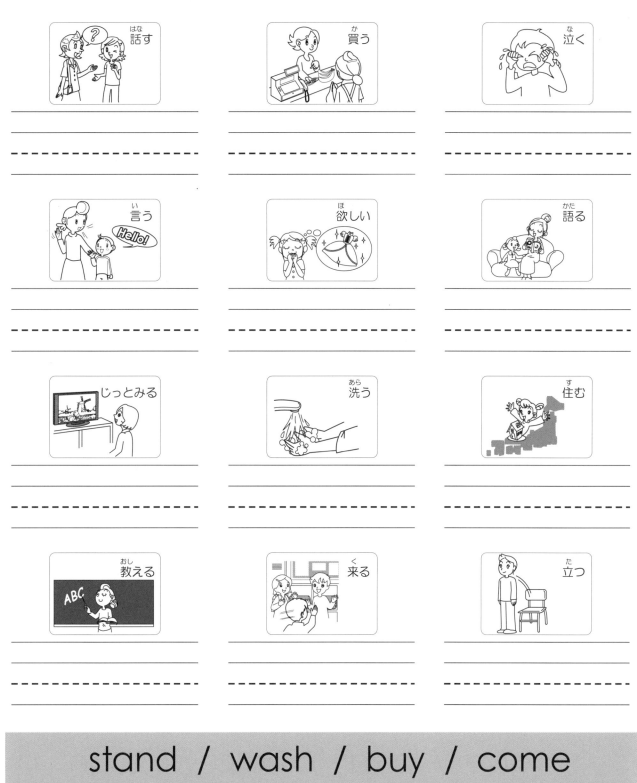

話す	買う	泣く
言う	欲しい	語る
じっとみる	洗う	住む
教える	来る	立つ

stand / wash / buy / come

live / speak / teach / want

tell / watch / cry / say

Choose the correct word from the ▨ and write it on the lines. （絵を見て、それが「どんな」動作か ▨ から選び線の上に書いてみよう！）

つか
使う

あ
会う

つ い
連れて行く

_____

- - - - - - - - - - -

_____

わら
笑う

わす
忘れる

なら
習う

_____

- - - - - - - - - - -

_____

あげる

てつだ
手伝う

ま
待つ

_____

- - - - - - - - - - -

_____

き
聞こえる

おく
送る

かんが
考える

_____

- - - - - - - - - - -

_____

give / hear / help / laugh

meet / use / send / forget

think / wait / learn / take

Choose the correct word from the ▨ and write it on the lines. （絵を見て、それが「どんな」動作か ▨ から選び線の上に書いてみよう！）

始める

_____

- - - - - - - - - - - - - - - - -

_____

感じる

_____

- - - - - - - - - - - - - - - - -

_____

見せる

_____

- - - - - - - - - - - - - - - - -

_____

失くす

_____

- - - - - - - - - - - - - - - - -

_____

持ってくる

_____

- - - - - - - - - - - - - - - - -

_____

見つける

_____

- - - - - - - - - - - - - - - - -

_____

話をする

_____

- - - - - - - - - - - - - - - - -

_____

もらう

_____

- - - - - - - - - - - - - - - - -

_____

掃除する

_____

- - - - - - - - - - - - - - - - -

_____

終わらせる

_____

- - - - - - - - - - - - - - - - -

_____

見える

_____

- - - - - - - - - - - - - - - - -

_____

知っている

_____

- - - - - - - - - - - - - - - - -

_____

begin / bring / feel / get
find / finish / know / lose
clean / see / talk / show

-27-

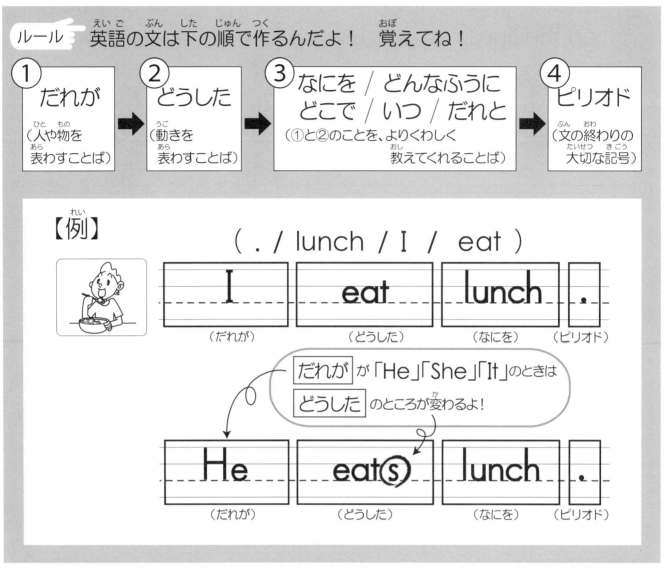

ルール　英語の文は下の順で作るんだよ！　覚えてね！

① だれが
（人や物を表わすことば）

② どうした
（動きを表わすことば）

③ なにを / どんなふうに どこで / いつ / だれと
（①と②のことを、よりくわしく教えてくれることば）

④ ピリオド
（文の終わりの大切な記号）

【例】

(. / lunch / I / eat)

I	eat	lunch	.
（だれが）	（どうした）	（なにを）	（ピリオド）

だれが が「He」「She」「It」のときは どうした のところが変わるよ！

He	eat(s)	lunch	.
（だれが）	（どうした）	（なにを）	（ピリオド）

Rearrange the words to make a sentence.
（次の英語を正しく並べかえて、絵に合う英語の文を作ろう！）

だれが が「He」「She」「It」のときは どうした のところの "～s, ～es"に注目しよう!!

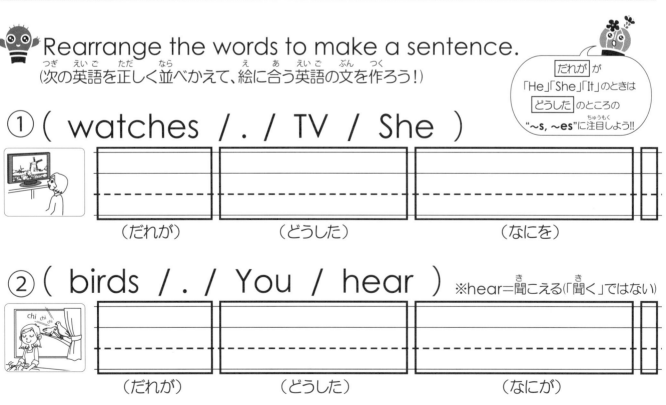

① (watches / . / TV / She)

（だれが）	（どうした）	（なにを）

② (birds / . / You / hear)　※hear＝聞こえる（「聞く」ではない）

（だれが）	（どうした）	（なにが）

Rearrange the words to make a sentence.
（次の英語を正しく並べかえて、絵に合う英語の文を作ろう！）

だれが が
「He」「She」「It」のときは
どうした のところの
"~s, ~es"に注目しよう!!

① (He / in Japan / . / lives)

（だれが）	（どうした）	（どこに）	

② (I / English / teach / .)

（だれが）	（どうした）	（なにを）	

③ (buys / . / She / bananas)

（だれが）	（どうした）	（なにを）	

④ (He / sells / . / vegetables)

（だれが）	（どうした）	（なにを）	

⑤ (laugh / at the TV / You / .)

（だれが）	（どうした）	（なにに）	

⑥ (learns / English / . / He)

（だれが）	（どうした）	（なにを）	

Let's read the sentences below. （次の文を読んでみよう!）

① I like strawberries.

② You like potatoes.

③ **He** likes tomatoes.

④ **She** likes bananas.

⑤ **It** likes carrots.

⑥ We like peaches.

⑦ You like mangoes.

⑧ They like grapes.

【例】 run
I run fast. （わたしは速く走ります）

He runs fast.
（彼は速く走ります）

go
I go to school. （わたしは学校に行きます）

She goes to school.
（彼女は学校に行きます）

fly
I fly in the garden. （わたしは庭を飛びます）

It flies in the garden.
（それは庭を飛びます）

Circle the correct words. （正しい英語に ◯ をつけよう!)

①  She (wash / washes) the dog.

②  He (cook / cooks) dinner.

③  It (sleep / sleeps) on the bed.

④  We (watch / watches) TV every day.

⑤  I (give / gives) you an apple.

⑥  They (play / plays) soccer.

⑦  You (run / runs) every day.

⑧ They (fly / flies) in the garden.

Complete the sentences. （　　に合うことばを入れて文を完成させよう！）

① She _____ the dog.

② He _____ dinner.

③ It _____ on the bed.

④ We _____ TV every day.

⑤ She _____ every day.

⑥ He _____ English.

⑦ I _____ a book.

⑧ I _____ juice.

英語の書き方がわからなければ
P22〜27を見てね！

① He _____ every day.

② They _____ soccer every day.

③ It _____ in the garden.

④ I _____ a letter.

⑤ She _____ you an apple.

⑥ You _____ the curtains.

⑦ He _____ a melon.

⑧ She _____ a dress.

英語の書き方がわからなければ
P22〜27を見てね！

Complete the sentences. （_____に合うことばを入れて文を完成させよう！）

① She _____ some food.

② He _____ vegetables.

③ It _____ a balloon.

④ They _____ the trees.

⑤ I _____ fast.

⑥ You _____ a bike.

⑦ It _____ high.

⑧ She _____ lunch.

英語の書き方がわからなければ
P22～27を見てね！

Complete the sentences. （_____に合うことばを入れて文を完成させよう！）

① I _____ the door.

② She _____ paper.

③ They _____ the mountain.

④ He _____ a map.

⑤ I _____ an eraser.

⑥ They _____ the class.

⑦ I _____ an eraser.

⑧ We _____ about the movie.

英語の書き方がわからなければ
P22〜27を見てね！

Complete the sentences. \quad（_____に合うことばを入れて文を完成させよう！）

① I _____ happy.

② She _____ that boy.

③ I _____ my recorder.

④ He _____ her to the park.

⑤ He _____ about lunch.

⑥ I _____ my friend.

⑦ We _____ the class.

⑧ She _____ her umbrella.

英語の書き方がわからなければ
P22〜27を見てね！

スペシャル問題！！
Special Challenge

Complete the sentences.
(_____に合うことばを入れて文を完成させよう！)

① わたしは学校に行きます。

_____ _____ to school.

② 彼女は絵を見ます。

_____ _____ at the picture.

③ 彼はピアノをひきます。

_____ _____ the piano.

④ わたしたちは英語を話します。

_____ _____ English.

⑤ 彼らは日本に住んでいます。

_____ _____ in Japan.

⑥ それは空を飛びます。

_____ _____ in the sky.

英語の書き方がわからなければ
P22〜27を見てね！

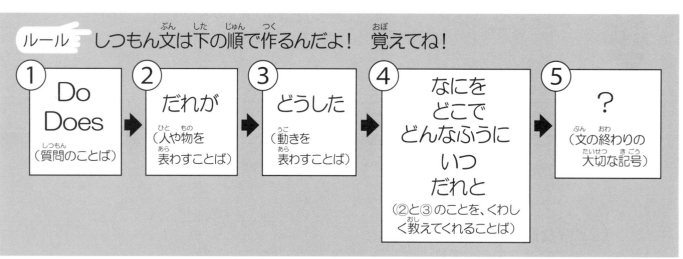

ルール しつもん文は下の順で作るんだよ！ 覚えてね！

①
Do
Does
（質問のことば）

②
だれが
（人や物を表わすことば）

③
どうした
（動きを表わすことば）

④
なにを
どこで
どんなふうに
いつ
だれと
（②と③のことを、くわしく教えてくれることば）

⑤
？
（文の終わりの大切な記号）

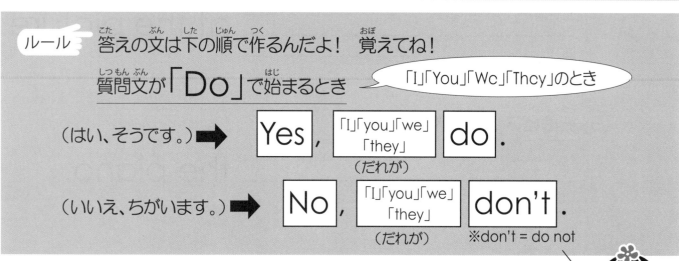

ルール 答えの文は下の順で作るんだよ！ 覚えてね！

質問文が「Do」で始まるとき ── 「I」「You」「Wc」「Thcy」のとき

（はい、そうです。）➡ Yes, 「I」「you」「we」「they」（だれが） do.

（いいえ、ちがいます。）➡ No, 「I」「you」「we」「they」（だれが） don't. ※don't = do not

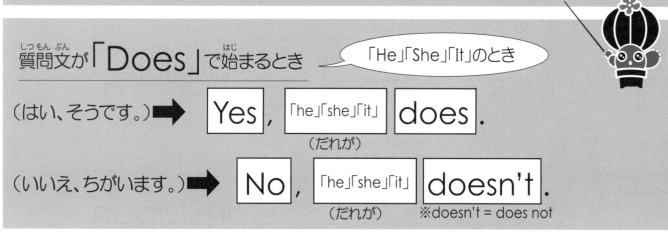

質問文が「Does」で始まるとき ── 「He」「She」「It」のとき

（はい、そうです。）➡ Yes, 「he」「she」「it」（だれが） does.

（いいえ、ちがいます。）➡ No, 「he」「she」「it」（だれが） doesn't. ※doesn't = does not

【例】Do you like apples? （あなたはりんごがすきですか？）

（はい、すきです）➡ Yes, I do.

（いいえ、すきではありません）➡ No, I don't.

Does she like apples? （かのじょはりんごがすきですか？）

（はい、すきです）➡ Yes, she does.

（いいえ、すきではありません）➡ No, she doesn't.

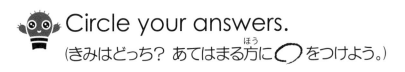

Circle your answers.

（きみはどっち？　あてはまる方(ほう)に◯をつけよう。）

①Do you like dogs?

(質問文(しつもんぶん))

（答(こた)えの文(ぶん)）　Yes, I do. / No, I don't.

②Do you like bananas?

Yes, I do. / No, I don't.

③Do you like monkeys?

Yes, I do. / No, I don't.

④Do you like cherries?

Yes, I do. / No, I don't.

⑤Do you like rabbits?

Yes, I do. / No, I don't.

⑥Do you like melons?

Yes, I do. / No, I don't.

⑦Do you like lions?

Yes, I do. / No, I don't.

⑧Do you like oranges?

Yes, I do. / No, I don't.

Write the missing words on the lines.

(　　に英語を書いて文を完成させよう！)

「Do」「Does」どちらが入るかな？
線に気を付けて書いてみよう！

(例) ① _Does_ she like dogs?

No, _she doesn't._

② _____ we like coffee?

Yes, _____

③ _____ I like watermelons?

Yes, _____

④ _____ it like carrots?

Yes, _____

⑤ _____ you like rice?

No, _____

⑥ _____ you like cherries?

Yes, _____

⑦ _____ he like onions?

No, _____

⑧ _____ they like milk?

Yes, _____

Write the correct words in the ☐.

（☐に正しい英語を書いて文を完成させよう！）

① ☐ she ☐ a book ?

Yes, she ☐ .

② ☐ he ☐ soccer ?

No, he ☐ .

③ ☐ you ☐ a letter ?

Yes, ☐ ☐ .

④ ☐ they ☐ the class ?

No, ☐ ☐ .

⑤ ☐ it ☐ the tree ?

Yes, ☐ ☐ .

⑥ ☐ he ☐ a bike ?

☐ , ☐ ☐ .

Write the correct words in the ☐.

（☐に正しい英語を書いて文を完成させよう！）

① _____ he _____ an eraser?

Yes, _____ _____ .

② _____ you _____ a map?

No, _____ _____ .

③ _____ she _____ an eraser?

Yes, _____ _____ .

④ _____ he _____ the mountain?

No, _____ _____ .

⑤ _____ they _____ the class?

Yes, _____ _____ .

⑥ _____ we _____ about the movie?

_____ , _____ _____ .

スペシャル問題！！
Special Challenge

Complete the questions by adding the correct question word and choosing the correct verb.

（正しい言葉を下から選んで ＿＿＿＿ の上に書き、文を完成させよう。
ただし、質問の時に使われる一語が不足しているので加えてね。）

① 彼女はさよならを言いますか？

＿＿＿＿ she ＿＿＿＿＿＿＿＿ "Goodbye"?

② 私たちは駅で会いますか？

＿＿＿＿ we ＿＿＿＿＿＿＿＿ at the station ?

③ 私は彼女を待ちますか？

＿＿＿＿ I ＿＿＿＿＿＿＿＿ for her ?

④ 彼らはその箱を持っていますか？

＿＿＿＿ they ＿＿＿＿＿＿＿＿ the boxes ?

⑤ 彼は毎日カバンを忘れますか？

＿＿＿＿ he ＿＿＿＿＿＿＿＿ his bag every day ?

⑥ あなたは彼女を公園に連れて行きますか？

＿＿＿＿ you ＿＿＿＿＿＿＿＿ her to the park ?

⑦ あなたは彼を知っていますか？

＿＿＿＿ you ＿＿＿＿＿＿＿＿ him ?

say / forget / know / have

meet / take / wait

-43-

Section 1　New!　do not / does not

否定を表わす文を作ろう do / does + not （～ではありません）

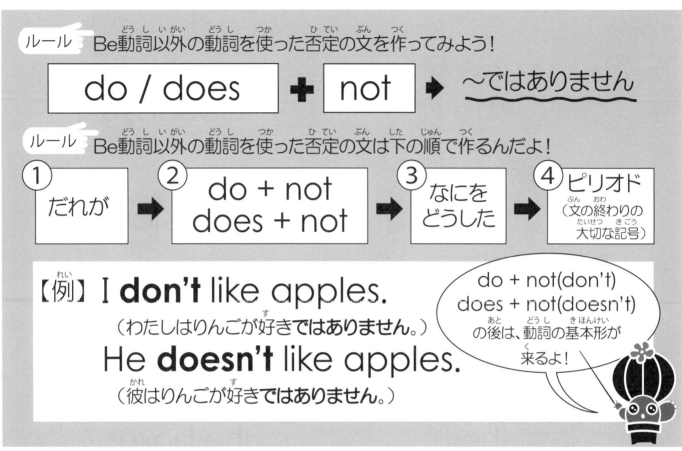

ルール　Be動詞以外の動詞を使った否定の文を作ってみよう！

$$do / does + not → ～ではありません$$

ルール　Be動詞以外の動詞を使った否定の文は下の順で作るんだよ！

① だれが　→　② do + not / does + not　→　③ なにを どうした　→　④ ピリオド （文の終わりの大切な記号）

【例】 I **don't** like apples.
（わたしはりんごが好きではありません。）
He **doesn't** like apples.
（彼はりんごが好きではありません。）

do + not(don't)
does + not(doesn't)
の後は、動詞の基本形が来るよ！

Let's read the sentences below. （次の文を読んでみよう！）

check

① I **don't** drink milk. ☐

② You **don't** feel well. ☐

③ He **doesn't** cook dinner. ☐

④ She **doesn't** read comic books. ☐

⑤ It **doesn't** eat rice. ☐

⑥ We **don't** laugh. ☐

⑦ You **don't** teach math. ☐

⑧ They **don't** meet at the hospital. ☐

1つに合体できる！ do not ➡ don't / does not ➡ doesn'tと、くっつけちゃう時もあるよ！

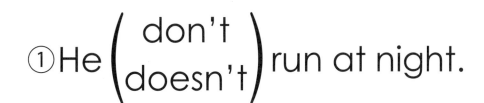 Circle the correct words. （正しい英語に◯をつけよう！）

① He (don't / doesn't) run at night.

② They (don't / doesn't) cut paper.

③ You (don't / doesn't) catch the ball.

④ I (don't / doesn't) sell vegetables.

⑤ We (don't / doesn't) draw pictures.

⑥ She (don't / doesn't) ride a bike.

⑦ You (don't / doesn't) teach English.

⑧ It (don't / doesn't) jump high.

Rearrange the words to make a sentence.

（（　）の言葉を並べかえて_____に正しい文を作ろう!）

文のはじめの文字は
大文字になるよ！

① 彼はロープを引きません。
(. / doesn't / he / pull / the rope)

② わたしは毎朝歩きません。
(walk / don't / every morning / I / .)

③ 彼らはその車を押しません。
(don't / they / . / the car / push)

④ わたし達は山を登りません。
(we / climb / don't / mountains / .)

⑤ 彼女は歌をうたいません。
(. / doesn't / she / songs / sing)

⑥ あなたは花にさわりません。
(touch / you / don't / flowers / .)

⑦ それはジャンプしません。
(it / jump / . / doesn't)

文のはじめの文字は
大文字になるよ！

（（　）の言葉を並べかえて＝＝＝に正しい文を作ろう！)

① わたしは上手におどりません。
(don't / I / dance / . / well)

----

② あなたはぼうしを持っていません。
(have / don't / a hat / you / .)

----

③ それは飛びません。
(doesn't / fly / . / it)

----

④ わたし達はテレビを見ません。
(TV / . / don't / we / watch)

----

⑤ 彼はお肉を買いません。
(meat / he / . / doesn't / buy)

----

⑥ 彼女は泣きません。
(cry / she / doesn't / .)

----

⑦ 彼らはその車を洗いません。
(wash / don't / the car / they / .)

 Write the sentences on the lines.

（_____ に英文を書こう！）

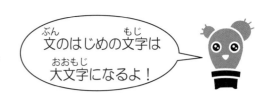
文のはじめの文字は
大文字になるよ！

① わたしはかさを持ってきません。

		I don't bring my umbrella.

② 彼らは宿題をしません。

		do their homework.

③ 彼はコンピューターを使いません。

		use a computer.

④ 彼女は彼の名前を忘れません。

		forget his name.

⑤ わたし達は歴史を習いません。

		learn history.

⑥ あなたは彼にアイスクリームをあげません。

		give him ice cream.

 Write the sentences on the lines.

（========= に英文を書こう!）

文のはじめの文字は
大文字になるよ！

① あなたはその本を見つけません。

find the book.

② 彼らは家をそうじしません。

clean the house

③ わたしは彼女を知りません。

know her.

④ 彼はわたしに写真を見せません。

show me the pictures

⑤ わたし達はプレゼントをもらいません。

get presents.

⑥ 彼女はわたしに話しをしません。

talk to me.

過去(終わったこと)を表わす動詞

過去
past ← | 今
now | → 未来
future

↑ 上の ▨ で行なわれたことは過去(終わったこと)のことだね。
それを表わす英語をここでは練習しよう!

過去(終わったこと)を表わす時は

『ごはんを きのう 食べる。』とは言わないね。➡ 『食べた。』になるよね。

英語も終わったことを表わす時は言葉が少し変わるんだよ!

≪時を表わすことば≫

ルール 次のことばが文中にあったら『過去(終わったこと)』を表わしているんだよ。

yesterday	(きのう)
last night	(きのうの夜)
last Monday	(先週の月曜日)
last week	(先週)
last month	(先月)
last year	(さく年／きょ年)
〜 ago	(〜前)

Choose the correct picture from Ⓐ to Ⓒ.
（次の文の表わす絵は下のどれかな？ Ⓐ～Ⓒから選んで◯をつけよう!）

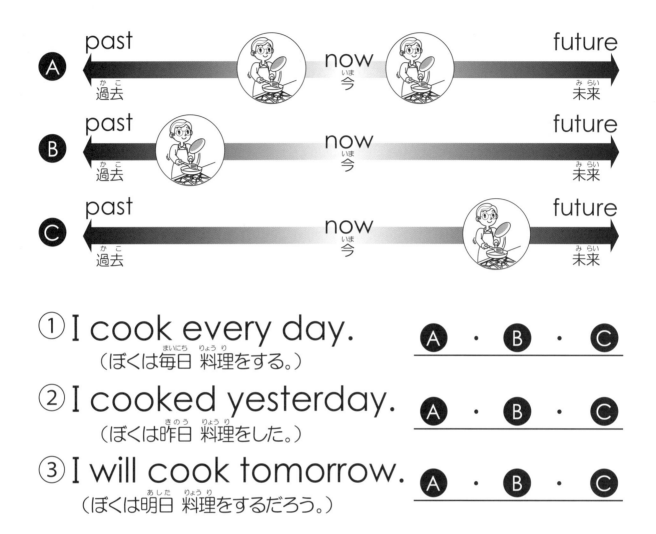

① I cook every day.
　（ぼくは毎日 料理をする。）　　Ⓐ ・ Ⓑ ・ Ⓒ

② I cooked yesterday.
　（ぼくは昨日 料理をした。）　　Ⓐ ・ Ⓑ ・ Ⓒ

③ I will cook tomorrow.
　（ぼくは明日 料理をするだろう。）　Ⓐ ・ Ⓑ ・ Ⓒ

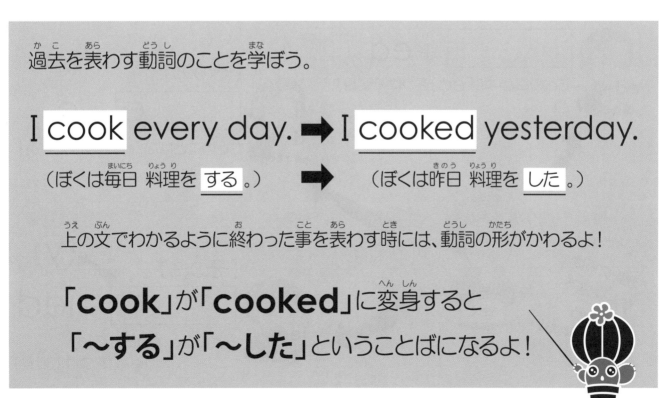

過去を表わす動詞のことを学ぼう。

I cook every day. ➡ I cooked yesterday.

（ぼくは毎日 料理を する 。）　➡　（ぼくは昨日 料理を した 。）

上の文でわかるように終わった事を表わす時には、動詞の形がかわるよ!

「cook」が「cooked」に変身すると
「〜する」が「〜した」ということばになるよ!

-51-

過去を表わす動詞のことを学ぼう！

ルール

I cook**ed** yesterday.

ぼくは昨日 料理を**した**。（昨日の事だよ！）

≪動詞を過去のことばに変身することを助ける2人≫

「きそくクン」　　　　「ふきそくチャン」

【例】**きそくクン**の場合… **次の3つの形に変身!!**

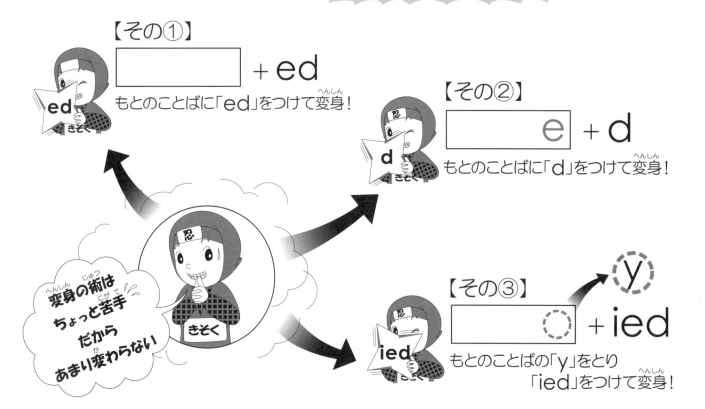

【その①】

☐ + ed

もとのことばに「ed」をつけて変身！

【その②】

☐ e + d

もとのことばに「d」をつけて変身！

変身の術は
ちょっと苦手
だから
あまり変わらない

【その③】

☐ ○ + ied → y

もとのことばの「y」をとり
「ied」をつけて変身！

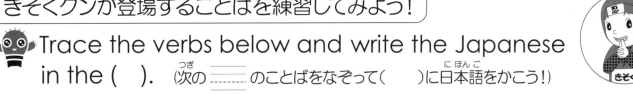

きそくクンが登場することばを練習してみよう！

Trace the verbs below and write the Japanese in the ( ).（次の ───── のことばをなぞって（　　）に日本語をかこう！）

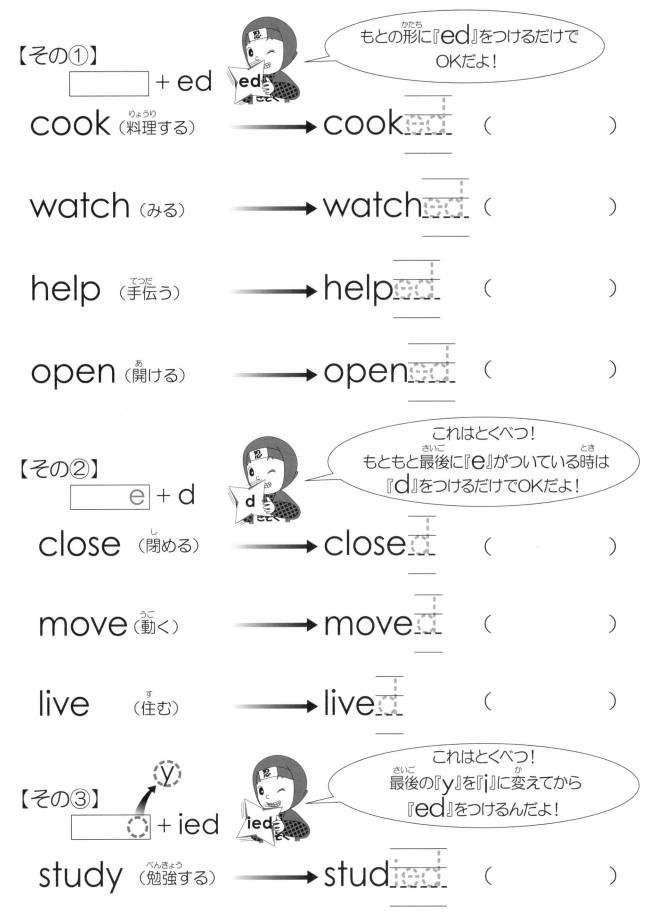

【その①】

　　□ + ed

もとの形に『ed』をつけるだけでOKだよ！

cook（料理する）　→　cooked（　　　　）

watch（みる）　→　watched（　　　　）

help（手伝う）　→　helped（　　　　）

open（開ける）　→　opened（　　　　）

【その②】

　　□ e + d

これはとくべつ！
もともと最後に『e』がついている時は『d』をつけるだけでOKだよ！

close（閉める）　→　closed（　　　　）

move（動く）　→　moved（　　　　）

live（住む）　→　lived（　　　　）

【その③】

　　□ + ied

これはとくべつ！
最後の『y』を『i』に変えてから『ed』をつけるんだよ！

study（勉強する）　→　studied（　　　　）

注意しよう！

ルール 「He・She・Itはへそまがり」って Grammar 3 で学んだよね。
だから、下のようになるのは覚えているかな？

He ~~walk~~ ⟶ He (walks)

She ~~walk~~ ⟶ She (walks)

It ~~walk~~ ⟶ It (walks)

でも過去形（終わった事を表わす）では「He」「She」「It」でも

動詞は全て同じように変身するんだよ！

【例】きそくクンの場合…

I walk ⟶ I walk**ed**

You walk ⟶ You walk**ed**

He walk**s** ⟶ He walk**ed**

She walk**s** ⟶ She walk**ed**

It walk**s** ⟶ It walk**ed**

We walk ⟶ We walk**ed**

They walk ⟶ They walk**ed**

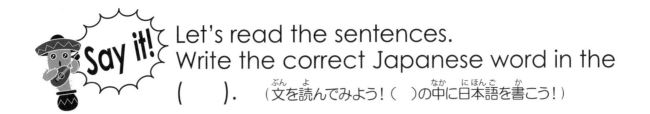

Say it! Let's read the sentences.
Write the correct Japanese word in the
( ). （文を読んでみよう！（ ）の中に日本語を書こう！）

① I help**ed** my mother yesterday.
( )

② You watch**ed** TV yesterday.
( )

③ He walk**ed** to school last year.
( )

④ She cook**ed** dinner last month.
( )

⑤ It open**ed** the door last night.
( )

⑥ We live**d** in Japan two years ago.
( )

⑦ You stud**ied** English last Monday.
( )

⑧ They use**d** the ball last week.
( )

【例】ふきそくチャンの場合…

go → went
行く / 行った

run → ran
走る / 走った

have → had
持つ / 持った

drink → drank
飲む / 飲んだ

eat → ate
食べる / 食べた

see → saw
見る / 見た

sit → sat
座る / 座った

come → came
来る / 来た

get → got
手に入れる / 手に入れた

write → wrote
書く / 書いた

わたしは変身が得意だから全く違う形に変われる！

覚えたかな？次のページからは自分で書くよ！なんども練習してみよう!!

ふきそくチャンが登場することばを練習してみよう！

🔹 Trace the verbs below and write the Japanese in the (　). （次の ＝＝＝ のことばをなぞって（　　）に日本語を書こう！）

go （行く） ➡ _went_ （　　　　　　）

run （走る） ➡ _ran_ （　　　　　　）

have （持つ） ➡ _had_ （　　　　　　）

drink （飲む） ➡ _drank_ （　　　　　　）

eat （食べる） ➡ _ate_ （　　　　　　）

see （見る） ➡ _saw_ （　　　　　　）

sit （座る） ➡ _sat_ （　　　　　　）

come （来る） ➡ _came_ （　　　　　　）

get （手に入れる） ➡ _got_ （　　　　　　）

write （書く） ➡ _wrote_ （　　　　　　）

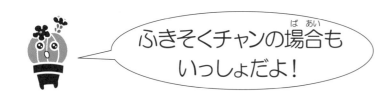

ふきそくチャンの場合も
いっしょだよ！

ルール 「He・She・Itはへそまがり」って Grammar 3 で学んだよね。
だから、下のようになるのは覚えているかな？

He go⨯ ⟶ He goes

She go⨯ ⟶ She goes

It go⨯ ⟶ It goes

でも過去形（終わった事を表わす）では「He」「She」「It」でも
動詞は全て同じように変身するんだよ！

【例】ふきそくチャンの場合…

変〜しん！

I go ⟶ I went

You go ⟶ You went

He go**es** ⟶ He went

She go**es** ⟶ She went

It go**es** ⟶ It went

We go ⟶ We went

They go ⟶ They went

Say it! Let's read the sentences.
Write the correct Japanese word in the
( ). (文を読んでみよう！（　）の中には日本語で書こう！)

① I **went** to school yesterday.
　(　　　　　)

② You **ran** in the park last week.
　(　　　　　)

③ He **had** a balloon yesterday.
　(　　　　　)

④ She **drank** some milk last night.
　(　　　　　)

⑤ It **ate** some food 30 minutes ago.
(　　　)

⑥ We **saw** the castle last year.
　(　　　　　)

⑦ You **sat** on the sofa yesterday.
　(　　　　　)

⑧ They **came** from China last week.
　(　　　　　)

Trace the verbs below and read the sentences.

（正しい形でなぞって書いたら、読んでみよう！）

ぼくが登場する時の
パターンを思い出してね！

① They <u>talk</u> about TV every day.

They __talked__ about TV <u>last night.</u>

② I <u>live</u> in Japan.

とくべつだったね！
『d』をつけるだけでOKだよ！

I __lived__ in Japan <u>last year.</u>

へそまがりの『s』は外して
『ed』をつけるんだよ！

③ She <u>wants</u> a new dress every day.

She __wanted__ a new dress <u>last week.</u>

④ You <u>learn</u> to play the piano every day.

You __learned__ to play the piano

<u>last Monday.</u>

Trace the verbs below and read
the sentences.
（正しい形でなぞって書いたら、読んでみよう！）

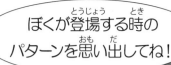 ぼくが登場する時の
パターンを思い出してね！

①I close the curtains every day.

I ___closed___ the curtains last night.

②We wash the dishes every day.

We ___washed___the dishes yesterday.

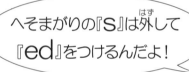 へそまがりの『S』は外して
『ed』をつけるんだよ！

③ He plays soccer every day.

He ___played___ soccer two days ago.

 enjoyも同じだよ！

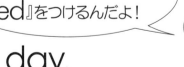 へそまがりの『S』は外して
『ed』をつけるんだよ！

④ She walks to school every day.

She ___walked___ to school yesterday.

Trace the verbs below and read the sentences.
(正しい形でなぞって書いたら、読んでみよう！)

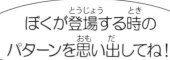
ぼくが登場する時の
パターンを思い出してね！

① She <u>opens</u> the box every day.

She _opened_ the box <u>last year.</u>

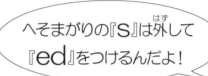
へそまがりの『s』は外して
『ed』をつけるんだよ！

② I <u>watch</u> TV every day.

I _watched_ TV <u>yesterday.</u>

へそまがりの『s』は外して
『ed』をつけるんだよ！

③ He <u>shows</u> the map every day.

He _showed_ the map <u>last Friday.</u>

④ You <u>pull</u> the dog every day.

You _pulled_ the dog <u>last night.</u>

Trace the verbs below and read the sentences.
（正しい形でなぞって書いたら、読んでみよう！）

 ぼくが登場する時の
パターンを思い出してね！

 きぞく

へそまがりの『s』は外すよ！

とくべつだったね！
『d』をつけるだけでOKだよ！

① She uses some glue every day.

She _____used_____ some glue last week.

とくべつだよね！

最後の『y』を『i』に変えてから
『ed』をつけるんだよ！
ied

② I study English every day.

I _____studied_____ English last year.

へそまがりの『s』は外すよ！

とくべつだったね！
『d』をつけるだけでOKだよ！

 d

③ He moves the chair every day.

He _____moved_____ the chair last month.

へそまがりの『s』は外して
『ed』をつけるんだよ！

④ She cooks dinner every day.

She _____cooked_____ dinner last night.

-63-

Trace the verbs below and read
the sentences.

（正しい形でなぞって書いたら、読んでみよう！）

わたしは
変身がとくい！
全然ちがう形に
変わるよ。

① She <u>runs</u> in the park every day.

She ‾‾‾‾ran‾‾‾‾ in the park <u>last year.</u>

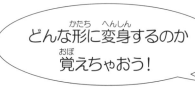

どんな形に変身するのか
覚えちゃおう！

② I <u>have</u> a class every day.

I ‾‾‾had‾‾‾ a class <u>yesterday.</u>

③ He <u>eats</u> curry and rice every day.

He ‾‾‾ate‾‾‾ curry and rice <u>last Friday.</u>

④ You <u>see</u> the dog every day.

You ‾‾‾saw‾‾‾ the dog <u>last night.</u>

Trace the verbs below and read the sentences.
(正しい形でなぞって書いたら、読んでみよう！)

① I <u>go</u> to school every day.
↘

I __went__ to school <u>last year.</u>

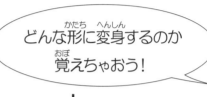

② She <u>drinks</u> some milk every day.
↘

She __drank__ some milk <u>30 minutes ago.</u>

③ He <u>sits</u> in the front seat every day.
↘

He __sat__ in the front seat <u>last Friday.</u>

④ You <u>write</u> a letter every day.
↘

You __wrote__ a letter <u>last night.</u>

ルール 今のことを質問する時は下の順で作るんだったね。覚えているかな?

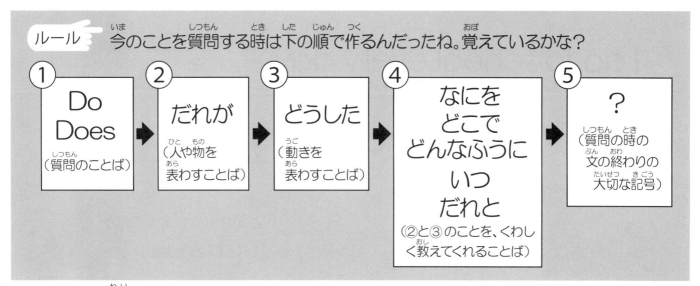

① Do Does （質問のことば）
② だれが （人や物を表わすことば）
③ どうした （動きを表わすことば）
④ なにを どこで どんなふうに いつ だれと （②と③のことを、くわしく教えてくれることば）
⑤ ? （質問の時の文の終わりの大切な記号）

【例】 Do **you** play soccer?
（あなたはサッカーをしますか?）

Does **he** play soccer?
（彼はサッカーをしますか?）

New!

ルール 終わったこと（過去）を質問する時も下の順で作るんだよ。覚えてね。

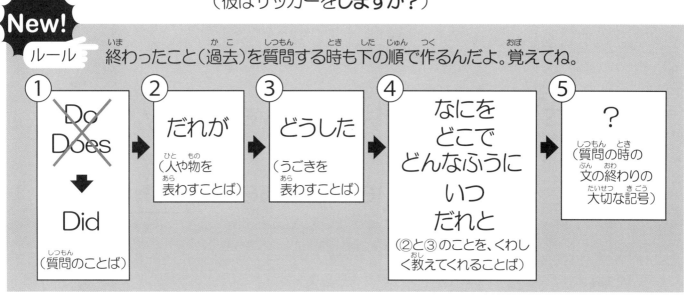

① ~~Do Does~~ ▼ Did （質問のことば）
② だれが （人や物を表わすことば）
③ どうした （うごきを表わすことば）
④ なにを どこで どんなふうに いつ だれと （②と③のことを、くわしく教えてくれることば）
⑤ ? （質問の時の文の終わりの大切な記号）

【例】 Did **you** <u>play</u> soccer?

Didサムライ参上!

～しましたか?

（あなたはサッカーをしましたか?）

Did **he** <u>play</u> soccer?

もとの形のままだよ!

✕ これはダメ! Did **he** play<u>ed</u> soccer?

≪質問文≫

Did が登場したら
cleaned ⇒ clean にもどるよ!
he, she, it でも clean❌ だよ!

I cleaned the room.
（わたしは部屋を掃除しました。）

 **Say it!** Let's read the sentences.
（文を読んでみよう!）

Didサムライ参上!

Did I clean the room?

Did you clean the room?

Did he clean the room?

Did she clean the room?

Did it clean the room?

Did we clean the room?

Did you clean the room?

Did they clean the room?

『Did〜?』は
『〜しましたか?』
という意味だよ!

へそまがりの『S』は
つかないよ!

≪質問文≫

Did が登場したら
ran ⇒ run にもどるよ！
he, she, it でも run✗だよ！

I <u>ran</u> in the park.
（わたしは公園を走りました。）

Say it! Let's read the sentences.
（文を読んでみよう！）

Didサムライ参上！

Did I <u>run</u> in the park?

Did you <u>run</u> in the park?

Did he <u>run</u> in the park?

Did she <u>run</u> in the park?

Did it <u>run</u> in the park?

『Did〜？』は
『〜しましたか？』
という意味だよ！

Did we <u>run</u> in the park?

Did you <u>run</u> in the park?

へそまがりの『S』は
つかないよ！

Did they <u>run</u> in the park?

Circle the correct words.

（正しいことばに ◯ をつけよう。）

『〜しましたか？』
と質問しているよ！

① Did <u>you</u> (study / studied) English **yesterday?**

基本の形の動詞を選んでね！！

② Did <u>she</u> (cooked / cook) dinner **last week?**

③ Did <u>he</u> (close / closed) the door **yesterday?**

④ Did <u>you</u> (use / used) the glue **yesterday?**

⑤ Did <u>they</u> (lived / live) in Japan **last year?**

⑥ Did <u>we</u> (wash / washed) the dishes **last night?**

 Circle the correct words.
（正しいことばに ◯ をつけよう。）

① Did <u>you</u> (talked / talk) to him **yesterday?**

 基本の形の動詞を選んでね！！

② Did <u>she</u> (walk / walked) to school **last week?**

③ Did <u>my brother</u> (play / played) soccer **yesterday?**

④ Did <u>they</u> (watched / watch) TV **last Monday?**

⑤ Did <u>you</u> (listened / listen) to the CD **yesterday?**

⑥ Did <u>my sister</u> (help / helped) him **last night?**

 Circle the correct words.
（正しいことばに ◯ をつけよう。）

『〜しましたか？』
と質問しているよ！

① Did <u>you</u> $\left(\begin{array}{c}\text{drink}\\\text{drank}\end{array}\right)$ orange juice
yesterday?

基本の形の動詞を選んでね！！

② Did <u>he</u> $\left(\begin{array}{c}\text{go}\\\text{went}\end{array}\right)$ to school **yesterday?**

③ Did <u>the cat</u> $\left(\begin{array}{c}\text{ran}\\\text{run}\end{array}\right)$ in the park
yesterday?

④ Did <u>we</u> $\left(\begin{array}{c}\text{saw}\\\text{see}\end{array}\right)$ the dog **last Monday?**

⑤ Did <u>you</u> $\left(\begin{array}{c}\text{eat}\\\text{ate}\end{array}\right)$ dinner **last night?**

⑥ Did <u>my uncle</u> $\left(\begin{array}{c}\text{wrote}\\\text{write}\end{array}\right)$ a letter
yesterday?

質問文が「Do」で始まるときは

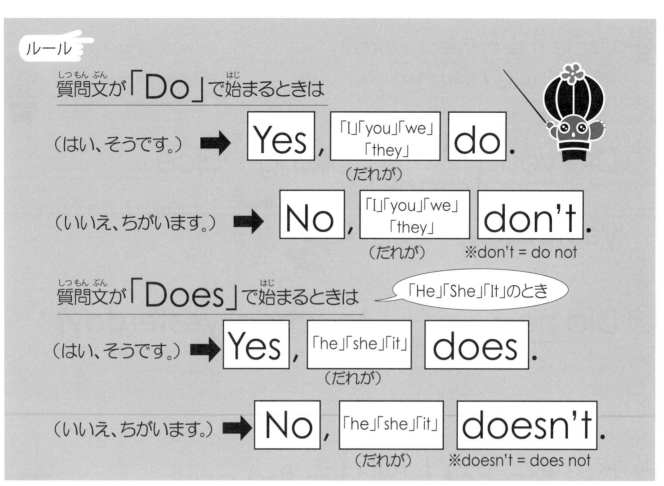

（はい、そうです。） ➡ **Yes**, 「I」「you」「we」「they」 **do**.
（だれが）

（いいえ、ちがいます。） ➡ **No**, 「I」「you」「we」「they」 **don't**.
（だれが） ※don't = do not

質問文が「Does」で始まるときは 「He」「She」「It」のとき

（はい、そうです。） ➡ **Yes**, 「he」「she」「it」 **does**.
（だれが）

（いいえ、ちがいます。） ➡ **No**, 「he」「she」「it」 **doesn't**.
（だれが） ※doesn't = does not

New!
質問文が「Did」で始まるとき

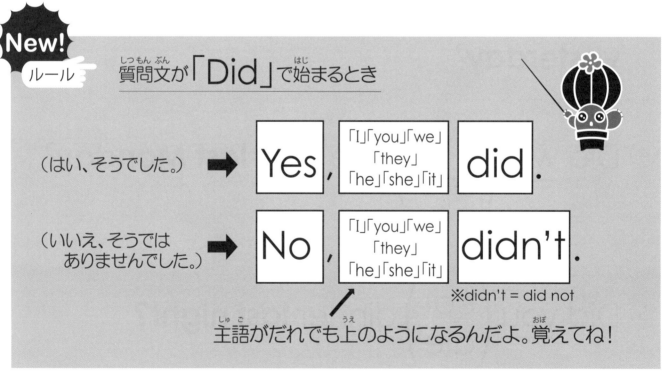

（はい、そうでした。） ➡ **Yes**, 「I」「you」「we」「they」「he」「she」「it」 **did**.

（いいえ、そうではありませんでした。） ➡ **No**, 「I」「you」「we」「they」「he」「she」「it」 **didn't**.
※didn't = did not

主語がだれでも上のようになるんだよ。覚えてね！

【例】Did you play soccer? （サッカーをしましたか？）

Yes, I **did**. （はい、しました。）

No, I **didn't**. （いいえ、しませんでした。）

 Let's read the sentences. (文を読んでみよう！)

【例】 Did you study yesterday?

Yes, I did.

No, I didn't.

(※didn't = did not)

 Complete the questions and circle the correct answers.
(_____ に合うことばを入れて文を完成させよう！ 正しい答えに ◯ をつけよう。)

① _____ you cook yesterday?

 Yes, I (did / didn't).

② _____ he walk to school yesterday?

 Yes, he (did / didn't).

③ _____ she watch TV yesterday?

 No, she (did / didn't).

④ _____ they sing a song yesterday?

 No, they (did / didn't).

Say it! Ask your friends the questions and circle their answers.

<ruby>友<rt>とも</rt></ruby><ruby>達<rt>だち</rt></ruby>に<ruby>次<rt>つぎ</rt></ruby>の<ruby>質問<rt>しつもん</rt></ruby>をしてみよう！ <ruby>答<rt>こた</rt></ruby>えに ◯ をつけてみよう！)

① Did you study yesterday?

> Yes, I did.

> No, I didn't.

② Did you eat lunch yesterday?

> Yes, I did.

> No, I didn't.

③ Did you watch TV yesterday?

> Yes, I did.

> No, I didn't.

④ Did you ride a bike yesterday?

> Yes, I did.

> No, I didn't.

⑤ Did you play baseball yesterday?

> Yes, I did.

> No, I didn't.

⑥ Did you read a book yesterday?

> Yes, I did.

> No, I didn't.

① ＿＿＿＿＿＿ you speak to her yesterday?

No, I $\left(\begin{array}{l} did \\ didn't \end{array}\right)$.

② ＿＿＿＿＿＿ she use some glue yesterday?

No, she $\left(\begin{array}{l} did \\ didn't \end{array}\right)$.

③ ＿＿＿＿＿＿ they swim yesterday?

Yes, they $\left(\begin{array}{l} did \\ didn't \end{array}\right)$.

④ ＿＿＿＿＿＿ you listen to the CD yesterday?

No, I $\left(\begin{array}{l} did \\ didn't \end{array}\right)$.

⑤ ＿＿＿＿＿＿ she learn to play the piano yesterday?

 Yes, she $\left(\begin{array}{l} did \\ didn't \end{array}\right)$.

 Circle the correct answers.

（正しい答えに ◯ をつけよう。）

① Did <u>you</u> give a present last year?

 あなたは〜？

Yes, (I did / you didn't).

はい、わたしは〜

② Did <u>she</u> run to school last week?

No, (he did / she didn't).

③ Did <u>my uncle</u> sing yesterday?

「uncle」は「おじさん」だよ！

Yes, (he did / we didn't).

④ Did <u>they</u> make a cake last Monday?

No, (we did / they didn't).

⑤ Did <u>my aunt</u> come to Japan two days ago?

Yes, (she did / he didn't).

「aunt」は「おばさん」だよ！

Complete the sentences. (===== に合うことばを入れて文を完成させよう！)

① __Did__ they play soccer yesterday?

Yes, __they did.__

② _____ you watch TV yesterday?

Yes, _____

③ _____ he find an eraser yesterday?

Yes, _____

④ __Did__ she wash the dishes yesterday?

No, __she didn't__

⑤ _____ you sell vegetables yesterday?

No, _____

⑥ _____ they talk yesterday?

No, _____

-77-

Complete the sentences. （ _____ に合うことばを入れて文を完成させよう！）

① Did you learn to play the piano yesterday?

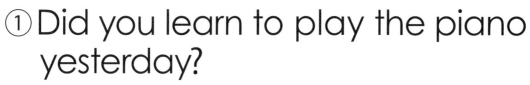 Yes, _____

② Did you forget your book yesterday?

 No, _____

③ Did you hear birds yesterday?

 No, _____

④ Did you listen to the CD yesterday?

 Yes, _____

⑤ Did you close the curtains yesterday?

 Yes, _____

⑥ Did you pick flowers yesterday?

 Yes, _____

Write the sentences on the lines.

（━━━━ に英文を書こう！）

文のはじめの文字は
大文字になるよ！

① 彼は窓を開けましたか？

| | | | the windows? |

② あなたは宿題を終わらせましたか？

| | | | your homework!? |

③ 彼女は手紙を送りましたか？

| | | | a letter? |

④ あなた達は野球をしましたか？

| | | | baseball? |

⑤ それは高く飛びましたか？

| | | | high? |

⑥ 彼らは野菜を売りましたか？

| | | | vegetables? |

否定を表わす文を作ろう その3 **did + not** （〜ではありませんでした）

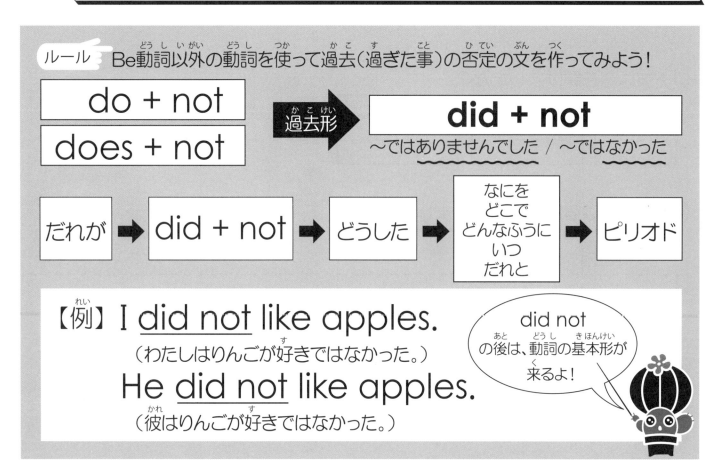

ルール Be動詞以外の動詞を使って過去（過ぎた事）の否定の文を作ってみよう！

do + not
does + not

過去形 → **did + not**
〜ではありませんでした / 〜ではなかった

だれが → did + not → どうした → なにを どこで どんなふうに いつ だれと → ピリオド

【例】 I <u>did not</u> like apples.
（わたしはりんごが好きではなかった。）
He <u>did not</u> like apples.
（彼はりんごが好きではなかった。）

did not の後は、動詞の基本形が来るよ！

Let's read the sentences below. （次の文を読んでみよう！）

check

① I **didn't** <u>drink</u> milk.

② You **didn't** <u>feel</u> well.

③ He **didn't** <u>cook</u> dinner.

④ She **didn't** <u>read</u> comic books.

⑤ It **didn't** <u>eat</u> rice.

⑥ We **didn't** <u>laugh</u>.

⑦ You **didn't** <u>teach</u> math.

⑧ They **didn't** <u>meet</u> at the hospital.

豆知識 did not ➡ didn't で使う事が多いよ！

Trace the words and read the sentences.
（点線の英語をなぞってから、文を読んでみよう！）

① I opened the box. ⟶

I [didn't] [open] the box.

② You threw the ball. ⟶

You [didn't] [throw] the ball.

③ He walked around the lake. ⟶

He [didn't] [walk] around the lake.

④ She drank coffee. ⟶

She [didn't] [drink] coffee.

⑤ It ate food. ⟶

It [didn't] [eat] food.

⑥ We taught English. ⟶

We [didn't] [teach] English.

⑦ They studied science.

They [didn't] [study] science.

Use "didn't" and rewrite the sentences.
（「didn't」を使って否定形の文を完成させよう！）

① I lived in Tokyo. ⟶

I ☐ ☐ in Tokyo.

② You watched TV last night. ⟶

You ☐ ☐ TV last night.

③ He forgot his homework. ⟶

He ☐ ☐ his homework.

④ She played the piano. ⟶

She ☐ ☐ the piano.

⑤ It ran fast. ⟶

It ☐ ☐ fast.

⑥ We washed the dishes. ⟶

We ☐ ☐ the dishes.

⑦ They came to my house.

They ☐ ☐ to my house.

① わたしは窓を閉めませんでした。
(didn't / close / I / the window / .)

② あなたは音楽を聞いていませんでした。
(listen / to music / didn't / . / you)

③ 彼はくだものを売りませんでした。
(sell / didn't / . / he / fruit)

④ 彼女は夕食を作りませんでした。
(cook / didn't / she / . / dinner)

⑤ それは海に住んでいませんでした。
(didn't / . / it / in the sea / live)

⑥ わたし達はそのレストランを見つけませんでした。
(didn't / we / the restaurant / . / find)

⑦ 彼らはその山に登りませんでした。
(climb / didn't / . / they / the mountain)

新しい動詞の紹介

Grammar 5
からの新しい動詞だよ！
覚えてね！

Match the pictures to the English sentences.
（絵にあった英語の文を選んで線で結ぼう！）

① I **carry** the box.　　●

（楽しむ）

② It **grows** every day.　　●

（運ぶ）

③ I **enjoy** my dessert.　　●

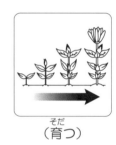
（育つ）

④ I **hurt** my leg.　　●

（電話する）

⑤ I **choose** an orange.　●

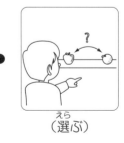
（選ぶ）

⑥ I **call** my friend.　　●

Ouch!
（けがをする）

Match the pictures to the English sentences.（絵にあった英語の文を選んで線で結ぼう！）

Grammar 5
からの新しい動詞だよ！
覚えてね！

① I **break** a vase. •

（落ちる）

② I **count** the apples. •

（決める）

③ I **fall** down the stairs. •

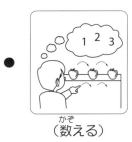
（数える）

④ I **hit** a punching bag. •

（こわす）

⑤ I **decide** to buy white shoes. •

（招待する）

⑥ I **invite** my friend to my house. •

（打つ）

-85-

Grammar 5
からの新しい動詞だよ！
覚えてね！

Match the pictures to the English sentences.（絵にあった英語の文を選んで線で結ぼう！）

① I **arrive** at the port. •

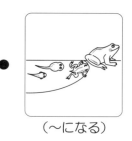
（～になる）

② It **becomes** a frog. •

とうちゃく
（到着する）

③ I **build** a house. •

おとず
（訪れる）

④ I **visit** my friend's house. •

うんてん
（運転する）

⑤ I **leave** my house. •

た
（建てる）

⑥ I **drive** to school. •

しゅっぱつ
（出発する）

Say it! Choose the correct word from the ▢ and write it on the lines. Then read the sentences.

（絵を見て、それが「どんな」動作か ▢ から選び線の上に書いてみよう！
それから英文を読んでみよう！）

① I _____ to school.

② It _____ every day.

③ She _____ at the port.

④ He _____ a house.

⑤ I _____ an orange.

⑥ I _____ a vase.

〜s がつく言葉があるね。
なぜついているのか
考えてね！

drive / arrives / grows
builds / break / choose

-87-

Say it! Choose the correct word from the ▮ and
write it on the lines. Then read the sentences.
（絵を見て、それが「どんな」動作か ▮ から選び線の上に書いてみよう!
それから英文を読んでみよう!）

① He ＿＿＿＿＿＿＿ the apples.

② It ＿＿＿＿＿＿＿ from the tree.

③ I ＿＿＿＿＿＿＿ to buy
white shoes.

④ I ＿＿＿＿＿＿＿ him in.

⑤ She ＿＿＿＿＿＿＿ my house.

⑥ It ＿＿＿＿＿＿＿ a frog.

〜S がつく言葉があるね。
なぜついているのか
考えてね!

counts / leaves / invite
decide / falls / becomes

Say it! Choose the correct word from the ☐ and write it on the lines. Then read the sentences.

（絵を見て、それが「どんな」動作か ☐ から選び線の上に書いてみよう！
それから英文を読んでみよう！）

① He _____ me.

② I _____ the box.

③ He _____ his dessert.

④ She _____ her leg.

⑤ She _____ her friend.

⑥ I _____ a punching bag.

～s がつく言葉があるね。
なぜついているのか
考えてね！

hit / visits / carry
hurts / calls / enjoys

Trace the verbs below and read.
Then write the Japanese in the (　).
（正しい形でなぞって読んでみよう！また、（　）に意味を書こう！）

ぼくが登場する時の
パターンを思い出してね！

① arrive ➝ arrived （　　　　　　　）

② call ➝ called （　　　　　　　）

③ carry ➝ carried （　　　　　　　）

④ count ➝ counted （　　　　　　　）

⑤ invite ➝ invited （　　　　　　　）

⑥ decide ➝ decided （　　　　　　　）

⑦ enjoy ➝ enjoyed （　　　　　　　）

playと同じだよ！

⑧ visit ➝ visited （　　　　　　　）

Trace the verbs below and read. 変〜しん！
Then write the Japanese in the (　).

（ 正しい形でなぞって読んでみよう！また、(　)に意味を書こう! ）

① become ⟶ became (　　　　　　)

② break ⟶ broke (　　　　　　)

③ build ⟶ built (　　　　　　)

④ drive ⟶ drove (　　　　　　)

⑤ fall ⟶ fell (　　　　　　)

⑥ grow ⟶ grew (　　　　　　)

⑦ hit ⟶ hit (　　　　　　)

⑧ hurt ⟶ hurt (　　　　　　)

⑨ leave ⟶ left (　　　　　　)

⑩ choose ⟶ chose (　　　　　　)

Circle the correct words.
（正しいことばに ◯ をつけよう。）

① She $\begin{pmatrix} \text{arrive} \\ \text{arrives} \\ \text{arrived} \end{pmatrix}$ in Tokyo yesterday.

② They $\begin{pmatrix} \text{build} \\ \text{builds} \\ \text{built} \end{pmatrix}$ my house last year.

③ He $\begin{pmatrix} \text{drive} \\ \text{drives} \\ \text{drove} \end{pmatrix}$ to school every day.

『今』の事だよ！

④ I $\begin{pmatrix} \text{invite} \\ \text{invites} \\ \text{invited} \end{pmatrix}$ my friends to the concert last month.

⑤ We $\begin{pmatrix} \text{carry} \\ \text{carries} \\ \text{carried} \end{pmatrix}$ some boxes yesterday.

⑥ You $\begin{pmatrix} \text{fall} \\ \text{falls} \\ \text{fell} \end{pmatrix}$ from the roof a week ago.

 Circle the correct words.
（正しいことばに◯をつけよう。）

『今』の事だよ！

① It
$$\begin{pmatrix} grow \\ grows \\ grew \end{pmatrix}$$
every day.

② I
$$\begin{pmatrix} stay \\ stays \\ stayed \end{pmatrix}$$
at the hotel last night.

『今』の事だよ！

③ We
$$\begin{pmatrix} call \\ calls \\ called \end{pmatrix}$$
her mother every morning.

④ She
$$\begin{pmatrix} visit \\ visits \\ visited \end{pmatrix}$$
my home yesterday.

⑤ They
$$\begin{pmatrix} choose \\ chooses \\ chose \end{pmatrix}$$
the house a year ago.

『今』の事だよ！

⑥ You
$$\begin{pmatrix} enjoy \\ enjoys \\ enjoyed \end{pmatrix}$$
the lessons every day.

Be動詞 + 動詞 + ing は『今 〜しています』という表現だったね。覚えてるかな？

【例】I **am washing** my hands.

（わたしは 今、手をあらっています。）

He **is playing** soccer.

（かれは 今、サッカーをしています。）

『動詞 + ing』にした時、動詞の形がかわるもの

Trace the letters and read the sentences.

（点線の文字をなぞってから文を読んでみよう！）

ルール　動詞の最後に『 e 』がつく単語は『 e 』をとって『 ing 』をつける

① write → writ~~e~~ing

I __am__ writ~~e~~ing a letter.

② make → mak~~e~~ing

We __are__ mak~~e~~ing a cake.

ルール　動詞の最後の文字が重なる

① run + n + ing → running

You __are__ running in the park.

② cut + t + ing → cutting

She __is__ cutting paper.

Complete the sentences. (_____ に合うことばを入れて文を完成させよう！)

①  He __is__ push__ing__ the ball.

②  She _____ touch_____ the wall.

③  You _____ open_____ the curtains.

④  It _____ sleep_____.

⑤  They _____ play_____ soccer.

⑥  I _____ cook_____.

⑦  We _____ look_____ at a picture.

⑧  I _____ climb_____ a tree.

⑨  You _____ jump_____ on the bed.

Say it! Choose the correct word from the ⬜ and write it on the lines. Then read the sentences.

（絵を見て、それが「どんな」動作か⬜から選び、正しい形で線の上に書いてみよう！それから英文を読んでみよう！）

① ぼくは今、ミルクを飲んでいます。

I _____ _____ milk.

② 彼は今、木に登っています。

He _____ _____ a tree.

③ 彼女は今、花をつんでいます。

She _____ _____ a flower.

④ 彼らは今、りんごを数えています。

They _____ _____ apples.

⑤ あなたは今、絵を見せています。

You _____ _____ a picture.

⑥ わたしたちは今、家をそうじしています。

We _____ _____ our house.

climb / pick / drink
count / show / clean

「〜しています」は「〜ing」が動詞に付くよ！

-96-

① それは**今**、草を食べ**ています**。

It _____ _____ some grass.

② わたしたちは**今**、歌を歌っ**ています**。

We _____ _____ songs.

③ 彼は**今**、バスを待っ**ています**。

He _____ _____ for a bus.

④ 彼女は**今**、お昼ごはんを料理し**ています**。

She _____ _____ lunch.

⑤ ぼくは**今**、ベットで寝**ています**。

I _____ _____ in bed.

⑥ 彼女らは**今**、お皿を洗っ**ています**。

They _____ _____ the dishes.

---

sing / cook / sleep
eat / wait / wash

「〜しています」は
「〜ing」が動詞に付くよ！

 Complete the sentences.
（_____に合うことばを入れて文を完成させよう！）

 「He / She / It」は
どうするんだっけ？

① You _____ every day. （あなたは毎日あるきます。）

② You ____ _____. （あなたは今、あるいています。）

③ He _____ soccer every day.
（彼は毎日サッカーをします。）

④ He ____ _____ soccer.
（彼は今、サッカーをしています。）

⑤ She _____ every day. （彼女は毎日料理をします。）

⑥ She ____ _____. （彼女は今、料理をしています。）

⑦ It _____ every day. （それは毎日走ります。）

⑧ It ____ _____. （それは今、走っています。）

⑨ We _____ pictures every day.
（わたしはちは毎日絵を描きます。）

⑩ We ____ _____ pictures.
（わたしはちは今、絵を描いています。）

スペシャル問題！！
Special Challenge

Complete the sentences to make a conversation.
（＿＿＿＿に合うことばを入れて会話文を完成させよう！）

A: What are you doing?

B: ＿＿＿ ＿＿ ＿＿＿＿＿ English.

A: What ＿＿＿ you ＿＿＿＿＿ ?

B: ＿＿＿ ＿＿ ＿＿＿＿＿ TV.

A: What ＿＿＿ you ＿＿＿＿＿ ?

B: ＿＿＿ ＿＿ ＿＿＿＿＿ soccer.

A: What ＿＿＿ you ＿＿＿＿＿ ?

B: ＿＿＿ ＿＿ ＿＿＿＿＿ a book.

P100~109は Grammar 2~4の 復習だよ！

Choose the correct word and write it on the lines.

（正しい言葉を下から選んで ───── の上に書こう！）

①The rabbit is ＿＿＿＿＿＿＿＿＿ the hat.

②The rabbit is ＿＿＿＿＿＿＿＿＿ the hats.

③The rabbit is ＿＿＿＿＿＿＿＿＿ the hat.

④The rabbit is ＿＿＿＿＿＿＿＿＿ the hat.

⑤The rabbit is ＿＿＿＿＿＿＿＿＿ the hat.

⑥The rabbit is ＿＿＿＿＿＿＿＿＿ the hat.

---

in / under / between

on / in front of / by

Choose the correct word and write it on the lines.
（正しい言葉を下から選んで ＿＿＿＿ の上に書こう！）

①The cat is ＿＿＿＿＿＿ the bag.

②The girl is ＿＿＿＿＿＿ the door.

③The boy is ＿＿＿＿＿＿＿＿ the tent.

④The turtle is ＿＿＿＿＿＿ the box.

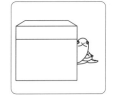

⑤The hospital is ＿＿＿＿＿＿＿＿＿＿ the house.

⑥The baskets are ＿＿＿＿＿＿ the door.

2回ずつ使ってね！

behind / far from / near

-101-

Write the correct Japanese on the line.
「うさぎ」はどこにいる？日本語の線のところに「うさぎ」のいる"ばしょ"を書いてみよう

"by"も
"next to"も
"beside"も
みんな意味は
似ているよ！

Where is the rabbit?
（うさぎはどこにいる？）

It is | by | the hat.

うさぎはどこにいる？
⟹ ぼうしの＿＿＿＿＿にいます。

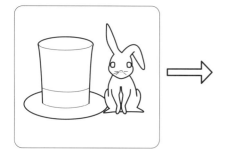

It is | next to | the hat.

うさぎはどこにいる？
⟹ ぼうしの＿＿＿＿＿にいます。

It is | beside | the hat.

うさぎはどこにいる？
⟹ ぼうしの＿＿＿＿＿にいます。

みんな意味は似ているよ！

by→そば ／ next to→となり ／ beside→となり

Trace the words and write the correct Japanese on the line.

（===の英語をなぞって文を完成させよう！英文と意味が合うように、日本語の文の_____ にも合う言葉を書こう！）

① Where are the pears?

They are _next to_ the fridge.

（ナシは冷蔵庫の_____です。）

② Where is the camera?

It is _by_ the computer.

（カメラはコンピューターの_____です。）

③ Where is the hospital?

It is _beside_ the station.

（病院は駅の_____です。）

スペシャル問題!!
Special Challenge

Look at the map and answer the questions by writing the correct words on the lines. （地図を見て問題に答えてみよう！　答えの文の ____ に当てはまる英語を書いてみよう！）

post office

police station

fire station

restaurant

school

hospital

hotel

park

supermarket

① What is next to the supermarket?

The _____ is next to the supermarket.

② What is by the park?

The _____ is by the park.

③ What is beside the hospital?

The _____ is beside the hospital.

【in / on / at】

ルール <u>in/on/at</u> は、場所を表わすこともできるけど『時間』を表わすことばの前にも使われるよ！
そして日本語の『～に』となるんだ。

下の英語を読んでみよう！

in 年・月・季節・午前中・午後などの前につくよ！

【例】 in 1998 （1998年に）
in May （5月に）
in the summer （夏に）
in the morning （午前中に）
in the afternoon （午後に）

on 曜日・日付などの前につくよ！

【例】 on July 2nd （7月2日に）
on Saturday （土曜日に）

at 時間などの前につくよ！

【例】 at seven （7時に）
at night （夜に）

日本語ではどの場合も同じ『～に』だけど、
英語では『in/on/at』と違うね。
上の文をセットで覚えてしまうといいよ！

Choose the correct word and write it on the lines.
(正しい言葉を下から選んで ＿＿＿＿ の上に書こう！)

①See you ＿＿＿＿＿ Friday!

②I get up ＿＿＿＿＿ seven every morning.

③Julia's birthday is ＿＿＿＿＿ August.

④What do you do ＿＿＿＿＿ Christmas Day?

⑤I play with my friend ＿＿＿＿＿ the afternoon.

⑥He watches TV ＿＿＿＿＿ night.

2回ずつ使ってね！

in / on / at

Circle the correct words. (正しいことばに ◯ をつけよう。)

① He goes to school (on / in / at) eight every day.

② Christmas Day is (on / in / at) December 25th.

③ I see stars (on / in / at) night.

④ George and I met (on / in / at) 2014.

⑤ We often go to the beach (on / in / at) the summer.

⑥ Let's meet (on / in / at) 7 o'clock tomorrow.

⑦ Did you go out (on / in / at) Thursday?

⑧ She moved to China (on / in / at) May.

⑨ She takes a piano lesson (on / in / at) Sundays.

【before / after / during】

ルール ☞ **before / after / during** は

『時』を表わすことばとして使われるよ!

下の英語を読んでみよう!

before 『〜の前』という意味

【例】 before the vacation （休みの**前に**）
before the movie 　（映画の**前に**）
before summer 　　（夏の**前に**）
before reading a book（読書の**前に**）

after 『〜の後』という意味

【例】 after the vacation （休みの**後に**）
after the movie 　（映画の**後に**）
after summer 　　（夏の**後に**）
after reading a book（読書の**後に**）

during 『〜の間』という意味

【例】 during the vacation （休みの**間に**）
during the movie 　（映画の**間に**）
during summer 　　（夏の**間に**）

Circle the correct words.
（正しいことばに ◯ をつけよう。）

① 映画の前に、私たちはお茶を飲みました。

$\left(\begin{array}{l}\text{Before} \\ \text{After} \\ \text{During}\end{array}\right)$ the movie, we had tea.

② 彼は会議の後に家に帰ります。

He goes home $\left(\begin{array}{l}\text{before} \\ \text{after} \\ \text{during}\end{array}\right)$ the meeting.

③ 夏休みの間に、私はアメリカへ行きました。

I went to America $\left(\begin{array}{l}\text{before} \\ \text{after} \\ \text{during}\end{array}\right)$ the summer vacation.

④ 彼女はお菓子を食べる前に手を洗いました。

She washed her hands $\left(\begin{array}{l}\text{before} \\ \text{after} \\ \text{during}\end{array}\right)$ eating snacks.

⑤ 夏の間に私たちはその山を登りました。

We climbed the mountain $\left(\begin{array}{l}\text{before} \\ \text{after} \\ \text{during}\end{array}\right)$ summer.

⑥ テスト前に彼らはいっしょうけんめいに勉強しました。

They studied hard $\left(\begin{array}{l}\text{before} \\ \text{after} \\ \text{during}\end{array}\right)$ the test.

様子を表わすことば

Match the pictures to the English sentences.
（絵にあった英語の文を選んで線で結ぼう！）

①  • • It is cloudy.

②  • • I am cold.

③  • • I am full.

④  • • It is sunny.

⑤  • • I am hungry.

⑥  • • I am hot.

⑦  • • It is windy.

⑧  • • It is rainy.

Match the pictures to the English sentences.
（絵にあった英語の文を選んで線で結ぼう！）

 ①　•

• He is tall.

 ②　•

• They are clean.

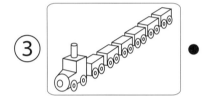 ③　•

• He is short.

 ④　•

• It is small.

 ⑤　•

• They are dirty.

 ⑥　•

• It is big.

 ⑦　•

• It is long.

 ⑧　•

• It is short.

Write the correct Japanese in the ☐.

（ ▓ のことばは人や物の"ようす"を表わすことばだよ。どんな"ようす"なのか ☐ の中に
日本語で書いてみよう！）

①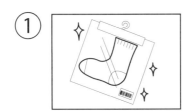

It is new.

それは ☐ です。

②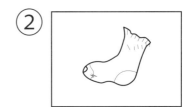

It is old.

それは ☐ です。

③

It is his left hand.

それは彼の ☐ 手です。

④

It is his right hand.

それは彼の ☐ 手です。

⑤

It is fast.

それは ☐ です。

⑥

It is slow.

それは ☐ です。

⑦

He is young.

彼は ☐ です。

⑧

He is old.

彼は ☐ です。

Write the correct Japanese in the ☐.

（■■のことばは人や物の"ようす"を表わすことばだよ。どんな"ようす"なのか ☐ の中に日本語で書いてみよう！）

①

It is good.

それは ☐ です。

②

It is bad.

それは ☐ です。

③

I am sad.

わたしは ☐ です。

④

I am happy.

わたしは ☐ です。

⑤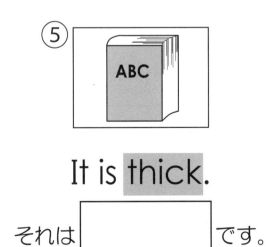

It is thick.

それは ☐ です。

⑥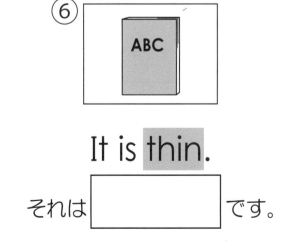

It is thin.

それは ☐ です。

Write the correct Japanese in the ☐.

（■■■ のことばは人や物の"ようす"を表わすことばだよ。
どんな"ようす"なのか ☐ の中に日本語で書いてみよう！）

Grammar 4
からの新しい言葉だよ！
覚えてね！

①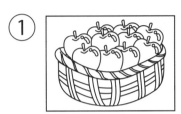

It is full.

それは ☐ です。

②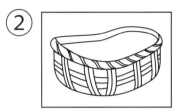

It is empty.

それは ☐ です。

③

It is easy.

それは ☐ です。

④

It is difficult.

それは ☐ です。

⑤

She is rich.

彼女は ☐ です。

⑥

She is poor.

彼女は ☐ です。

⑦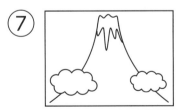

It is high.

それは ☐ です。

⑧

It is low.

それは ☐ です。

Write the correct Japanese in the ☐.

（ ▨ のことばは人や物の"ようす"を表わすことばだよ。
どんな"ようす"なのか ☐ の中に日本語で書いてみよう！）

Grammar 4
からの新しい言葉だよ！
覚えてね！

①

It is pretty.

それは ☐ です。

②

It is ugly.

それは ☐ です。

③

They are expensive.

それらは ☐ です。

④

They are cheap.

それらは ☐ です。

⑤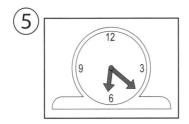

It is early in
the morning.

朝 ☐ です。

⑥

It is late at night.

夜 ☐ です。

Choose the correct word from the ▢ and write it on the lines. Then read the sentences.

（絵を見て、それが「どんな」様子か ▢ から選び線の上に書いてみよう！
それから英文を読んでみよう！）

① I am _____.

② It is _____.

③ I am _____.

④ It is _____.

⑤ It is _____.

⑥ They are _____.

⑦ She is _____.

big / long / short / windy
cold / new / hungry

Say it! Choose the correct word from the ▮ and write it on the lines. Then read the sentences.

（絵を見て、それが「どんな」様子か ▮ から選び線の上に書いてみよう！
それから英文を読んでみよう！）

① I am _____.

② He is _____.

③ It is _____.

④ They are _____.

⑤ I am _____.

⑥ It is _____.

⑦ It is _____.

rainy / old / happy / tall
cloudy / full / sunny

Say it!

Choose the correct word from the ▢ and write it on the lines. Then read the sentences.

（絵を見て、それが「どんな」様子か ▢ から選び線の上に書いてみよう！
それから英文を読んでみよう！）

① 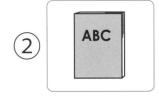 It is his _____ hand.

② 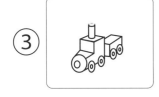 It is _____.

③  It is _____.

④  It is _____.

⑤ 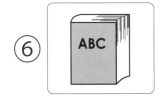 They are _____.

⑥  It is _____.

⑦ I am _____.

fast / sad / short / thin

hot / thick / left

-118-

Say it!

Choose the correct word from the ▮ and write it on the lines. Then read the sentences.

（絵を見て、それが「どんな」様子か ▮ から選び線の上に書いてみよう！
それから英文を読んでみよう！）

①  It is _____.

②  It is _____.

③  It is his _____ hand.

④  They are _____.

⑤  They are _____.

⑥  It is _____.

⑦  They are _____.

good / slow / clean / right
dirty / small / bad

Say it!

Choose the correct word from the ⬛ and write it on the lines. Then read the sentences.

（絵を見て、それが「どんな」様子か ⬛ から選び線の上に書いてみよう！
それから英文を読んでみよう！）

①  They are _____.

②  It is _____.

③  She is _____.

④  She is _____.

⑤  This homework is _____.

⑥  This test is _____.

expensive / rich / poor

difficult / easy / pretty

Say it! Choose the correct word from the ▪ and write it on the lines. Then read the sentences.

（絵を見て、それが「どんな」様子か ▪ から選び線の上に書いてみよう！
それから英文を読んでみよう！）

① 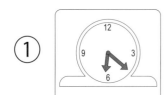 I get up _____ in the morning.

② 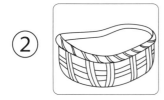 The basket is _____.

③  It is _____.

④  They are _____.

⑤ 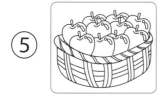 The basket is _____.

⑥  It is _____ at night.

cheap / full / late

early / empty / ugly

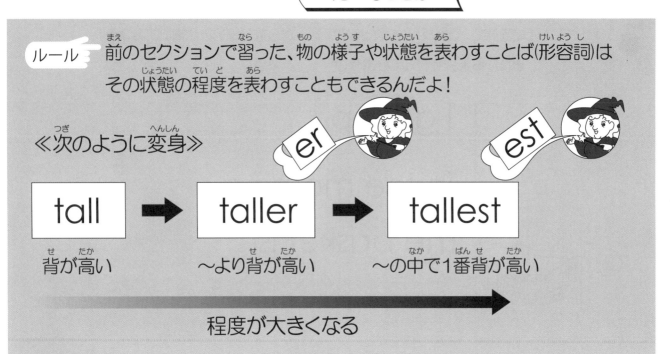

ルール 前のセクションで習った、物の様子や状態を表わすことば(形容詞)は
その状態の程度を表わすこともできるんだよ!

≪次のように変身≫

tall ➡ taller ➡ tallest

背が高い　　〜より背が高い　　〜の中で1番背が高い

程度が大きくなる

今までに習った形容詞は、みんな変身できるよ!

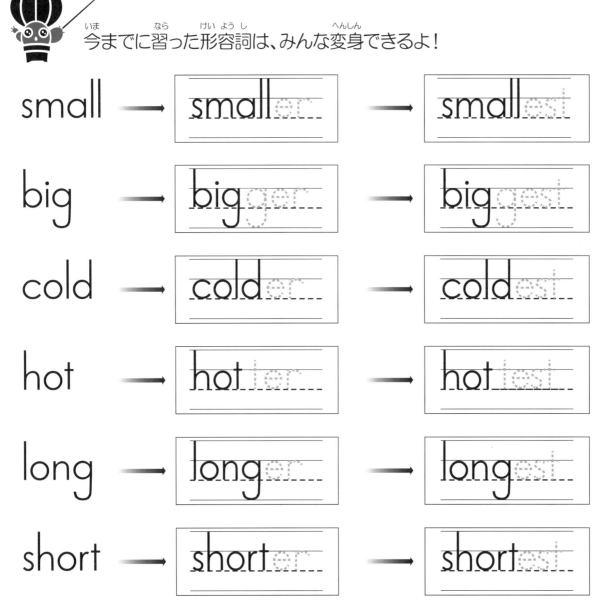

small	→	smaller	→	smallest
big	→	bigger	→	biggest
cold	→	colder	→	coldest
hot	→	hotter	→	hottest
long	→	longer	→	longest
short	→	shorter	→	shortest

Write the correct words.　（正しい英語を書こう！）

	～とくらべるともっと…だ	～の中で1番…だ
tall →		
small →		
big →		
cold →		
hot →		
long →		
short →		
old →		
young →		
high →		

くらべることば Part 1

ルール A と B をくらべる時には **than** (〜より)を入れて

A is tall<u>er</u> **than** B.

(A は B **より**背が高い。)

〜<u>er</u> **than** ☐ (☐ より 〜だ。)
(より)

Which is the winner? (次のくらべっこで勝者はどっち？　日本語で書いてみよう！)

① <u>Ken</u> is bigger **than** <u>Tom</u>.

Q：大きいのは・・・＿＿＿＿＿＿＿

② <u>The ruler</u> is longer **than** <u>that pencil</u>.

Q：長いのは・・・＿＿＿＿＿＿＿

③ <u>Spring</u> is colder **than** <u>summer</u>.

Q：寒いのは・・・＿＿＿＿＿＿＿

④ <u>Mt. Fuji</u> is higher **than** <u>Mt. Akagi</u>.

Q：高いのは・・・＿＿＿＿＿＿＿

⑤ <u>My hair</u> is shorter **than** <u>her hair</u>.

Q：短いのは・・・＿＿＿＿＿＿＿

⑥ <u>My car</u> is older **than** <u>your car</u>.

Q：古いのは・・・＿＿＿＿＿＿＿

Rearrange the words to make a sentence.

(（　）の言葉を並べかえて _____ に正しい文を作ろう!)

文のはじめの文字は
大文字になるよ!

① トムはケンより背が高い。

(Ken / **than** / is / Tom / taller / .)

_____

- -

② 春は夏より涼しい。

(spring / **than** / summer / . / is / colder)

_____

- -

③ 富士山は赤城山より高い。

(Mt. Akagi / is / higher / . / Mt. Fuji / **than**)

_____

- -

④ その定規はあの鉛筆より長い。

(that pencil / **than** / longer / the ruler / is / .)

_____

- -

⑤ ゾウはトラより大きい。

(**than** / a tiger / is / bigger / an elephant / .)

_____

- -

⑥ きみの車はぼくの車より古い。

(my car / **than** / older / your car / . / is)

_____

- -

ルール A の様子や状態が、あるグループの中で1番という時は

A is **the** tall<u>est</u> in the class.

(A はクラスの中で1番背が高い)

the ✚ ～<u>est</u> ➡ 1番～だ

Circle the correct words. (正しいことばに ◯ をつけよう。)

① Ken is **the** (short / shorter / shortest) in the class.

② Today is **the** (hot / hotter / hottest) day of the year.

③ This ruler is **the** (long / longer / longest) of all.

④ Mt. Fuji is **the** (high / higher / highest) mountain in Japan.

Write the correct Japanese on the line.
（次の英語を日本語にしよう！）

どんな様子か
日本語で書けるかな？

① Peter is taller than David.

_____ は _____ より _____ 。

② Mary is the youngest in the club.

_____ は _____ で一番 _____ 。

③ My sister is shorter than me.

_____ は _____ より _____ 。

④ Okinawa is hotter than Tokyo.

_____ は _____ より _____ 。

⑤ An airplane is bigger than a car.

_____ は _____ より _____ 。

⑥ Tokyo Skytree is the highest tower in Japan.

_____ は _____ で一番 _____ 。

 Circle the correct words.  （正しいことばに ◯ をつけよう。）

①I am (tall / taller / tallest) than Tom.

②He is the (young / younger / youngest) boy in the class.

③Hokkaido is (cold / colder / coldest) than Okinawa.

④Your hair is (long / longer / longest) than mine.

⑤Summer is the (hot / hotter / hottest) season in Japan.

⑥A *haiku* is the (short / shorter / shortest) poem in the world.

Rearrange the words to make a sentence.
(（　）内の言葉を並べかえて＿＿＿＿に正しい文を作ろう！)

① (Tom / **the** / is / tallest / in the class / .)

② (Hokkaido / is / **the** / in Japan / coldest place / .)

③ (My ruler / longest / is / . / **the** / in the class)

④ (Kagawa / is / **the** / smallest prefecture/ . / in Japan)

⑤ (Today / **the** / is / . / hottest day / of the year)

⑥ (Mary / **the** / . / shortest / is / in her family)

その1 ～います / ～あります

ルール　there はふつう『あそこ』という場所を表わすことばだね。

ところが there ＋ is / are になると

『あそこ』➡『います』『あります』という意味に変身!!

There is a pencil on the table.
（テーブルの上に1本の鉛筆があります。）

There are pencils on the table.
（テーブルの上に鉛筆が数本あります。）

上のように

There is ＋ a ➡ 『あるもの』、『いる人』が、1つまたは 1人の時は『There is』だよ!

There are ＋ ～s ➡ 『あるもの』、『いる人』が、2つまたは 2人以上の時は『There are』だよ!

① います あります ➡ ② なにが ➡ ③ どこに どんなふうに

Write the correct Japanese on the line.
（次の英語を日本語にしよう!）

① There is an egg in the basket.

バスケットに ＿＿＿＿＿ が ＿＿＿＿＿ 。

② There are tomatoes in the fridge.

冷蔵庫の中に ＿＿＿＿＿ が ＿＿＿＿＿ 。

Write the correct words on the lines and the correct Japanese.

（＿＿＿に正しい英語を書こう！ そして、英語を日本語にしよう！）

文のはじめの文字は大文字になるよ！

① ＿＿＿＿ ＿＿＿＿ **a boy** in the park.

（ 公園に ＿＿＿＿＿＿＿＿＿＿＿＿＿＿＿ ）

② ＿＿＿＿ ＿＿＿＿ **a piano** in the classroom.

（ 教室に ＿＿＿＿＿＿＿＿＿＿＿＿＿＿＿ ）

③ ＿＿＿＿ ＿＿＿＿ **many flowers** in the vase.

（ 花びんに ＿＿＿＿＿＿＿＿＿＿＿＿＿ ）

※many=「たくさん」という意味だよ！

④ ＿＿＿＿ ＿＿＿＿ **a pencil** in the bag.

（ かばんに ＿＿＿＿＿＿＿＿＿＿＿＿＿ ）

⑤ ＿＿＿＿ ＿＿＿＿ **two cats** by the window.

（ 窓辺に ＿＿＿＿＿＿＿＿＿＿＿＿＿＿＿ ）

⑥ ＿＿＿＿ ＿＿＿＿ **a pink car** on the street.

（ 道に ＿＿＿＿＿＿＿＿＿＿＿＿＿＿＿＿ ）

⑦ ＿＿＿＿ ＿＿＿＿ **five apples** in the basket.

（ バスケットに ＿＿＿＿＿＿＿＿＿＿＿ ）

Rearrange the words to make a sentence.

文のはじめの文字は大文字になるよ！

(（　）の言葉を並べかえて＿＿＿に正しい文を作ろう！)

① (a / there / in the tree / is / monkey / .)

② (on the wall / are / there / pictures / . / two)

③ (ball / is / under the table / . / there / a)

④ (an / there / on the desk / is / . / apple)

⑤ (carrots / on the plate / many / . / are / there)

※many=「たくさん」という意味だよ！

⑥ (six / in the bag / . / peaches / there / are)

Rearrange the words to make a sentence.

(( )の言葉を並べかえて ＝＝＝ に正しい文を作ろう!)

文のはじめの文字は大文字になるよ!

① (on the chair / an / there / orange / . / is)

_____

② (eraser / in my hand / an / is / there/ .)

_____

③ (many / in the zoo / animals / . / are / there)

_____

※many=「たくさん」という意味だよ!

④ (boy / a / is / in the classroom / . / there)

_____

⑤ (there / by the river / are / . / big trees)

_____

⑥ (a / there / star / is / . / in the sky)

_____

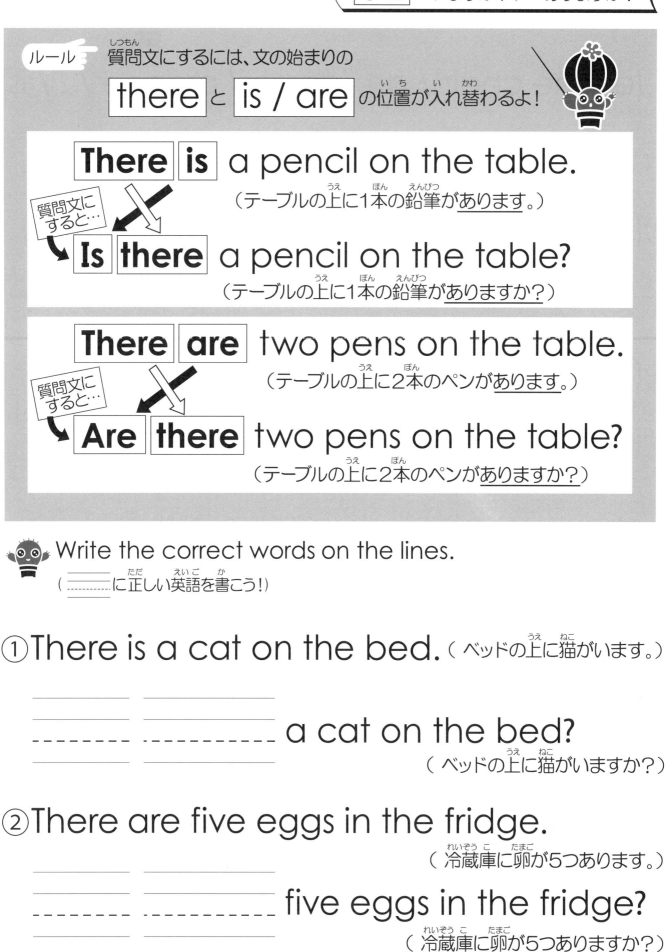

ルール　質問文にするには、文の始まりの

there と **is / are** の位置が入れ替わるよ！

There **is** a pencil on the table.
（テーブルの上に1本の鉛筆があります。）

質問文にすると…

Is **there** a pencil on the table?
（テーブルの上に1本の鉛筆がありますか？）

There **are** two pens on the table.
（テーブルの上に2本のペンがあります。）

質問文にすると…

Are **there** two pens on the table?
（テーブルの上に2本のペンがありますか？）

Write the correct words on the lines.
（＿＿＿に正しい英語を書こう！）

①There is a cat on the bed.（ベッドの上に猫がいます。）

＿＿＿＿ ＿＿＿＿ a cat on the bed?
（ベッドの上に猫がいますか？）

②There are five eggs in the fridge.
（冷蔵庫に卵が5つあります。）

＿＿＿＿ ＿＿＿＿ five eggs in the fridge?
（冷蔵庫に卵が5つありますか？）

Rearrange the words to make a sentence.

（（　）内の言葉を並べかえて ＿＿＿ に正しい文を作ろう！）

文のはじめの文字は
大文字になるよ！

① ベッドの上に猫がいますか？

(is / there / a / cat / ? / on the bed)

② かべに何枚かの写真がありますか？

(on / are / ? / the wall / there / pictures)

③ ふでばこの中に消しゴムが1個ありますか？

(eraser / there / an / is / in / ? /
the pencil case)

④ 図書館に本がありますか？

(are / in / the library / there / books / ?)

⑤ 箱の中にりんごがありますか？

(the box / apples / in / are / there / ?)

⑥ イスの下にクツはありますか？

(under / shoes / there / the chair / ? / are)

-135-

質問に対する答え方

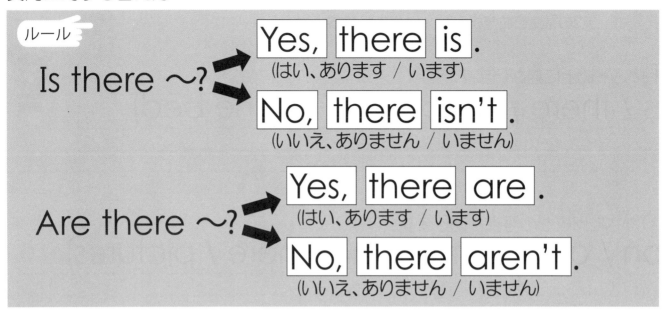

ルール

Is there ～?

→ Yes, there is .
（はい、あります / います）

→ No, there isn't .
（いいえ、ありません / いません）

Are there ～?

→ Yes, there are .
（はい、あります / います）

→ No, there aren't .
（いいえ、ありません / いません）

Complete the sentences. (＿＿＿ に合うことばを入れて文を完成させよう！)

①Is there a pumpkin on the table?

②Is there a girl by the tree?

③Are there pens on the desk?

④Are there trees in the park?

Write the missing words on the lines.

（_____ に英語を書いて文を完成させよう！）

【例】① __Is__ __there__ a pen on the desk?

No, __there isn't__

② _____ _____ two pens on the desk?

Yes, _____

③ _____ _____ a bird in the tree?

Yes, _____

④ _____ _____ ten ducks in the pond?

No, _____

⑤ _____ _____ five foxes on the log?

Yes, _____

⑥ _____ _____ a dog in the box?

Yes, _____

⑦ _____ _____ an eraser on the desk?

No, _____

⑧ _____ _____ three cats in the box?

Yes, _____

『できる』という意味の『can』は、動きを表わすことばと仲良しで出てくるよ！

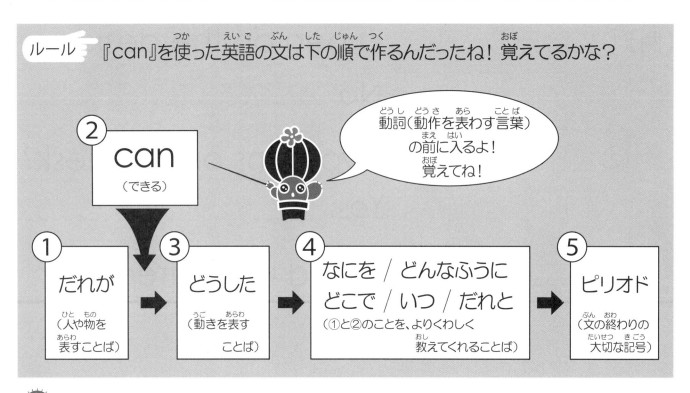

ルール 『can』を使った英語の文は下の順で作るんだったね！覚えてるかな？

Rearrange the words to make a sentence.
（（　）内の言葉を並べかえて ＿＿＿ に正しい文を作ろう！）

① (can / I / vegetables / . / eat)

（だれが）　（できる）　（どうすることが）　　（なにを）

② (He / open / can / the door / .)

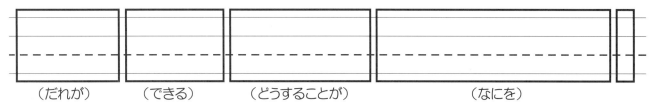

（だれが）　（できる）　（どうすることが）　　（なにを）

③ (read / They / . / English / can)

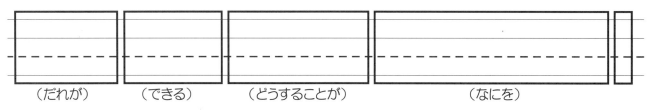

（だれが）　（できる）　（どうすることが）　　（なにを）

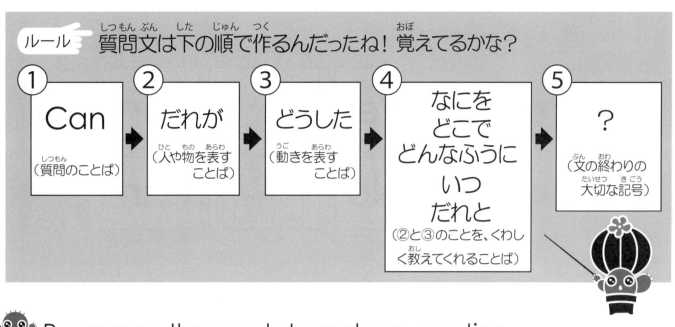

Rearrange the words to make a question.

（（　）内の言葉を並べかえて ――― に正しい文を作ろう！）

① (Can / I / vegetables / ? / eat)

（できる）　（だれが）　（どうすることが）　（なにを）

② (he / open / ? / Can / the door)

（できる）　（だれが）　（どうすることが）　（なにを）

③ (read / they / ? / English / Can)

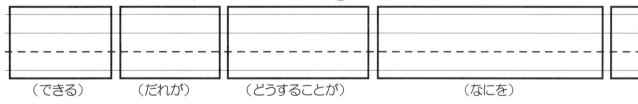

（できる）　（だれが）　（どうすることが）　（なにを）

④ (soccer / ? / Can / we / play)

（できる）　（だれが）　（どうすることが）　（なにを）

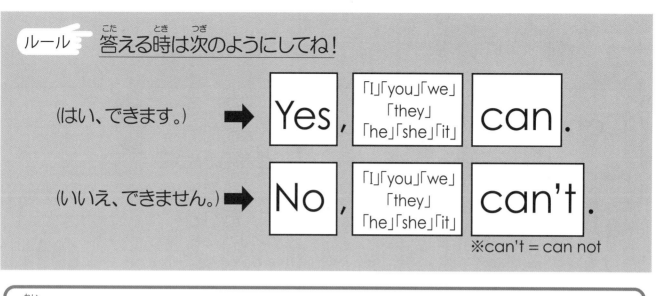

ルール 答える時は次のようにしてね！

(はい、できます。) ➡ Yes, [「I」「you」「we」「they」「he」「she」「it」] can.

(いいえ、できません。) ➡ No, [「I」「you」「we」「they」「he」「she」「it」] can't.

※can't = can not

【例】Can he play soccer? Yes, he can.

質問の時に使われる『人』か『もの』を入れてね。

Can you play tennis? No, I can't.

※ただし、質問の時に『You』で聞かれた時は『I』か『We』を入れてね。

Complete the sentences.（ ___ に合うことばを入れて文を完成させよう！）

① Can she ride a bike?

Yes, ___ ___ .

② Can they play soccer?

No, ___ ___ .

③ Can he drink milk?

Yes, ___ ___ .

④ Can you make a necklace?

Yes, ___ ___ .

-140-

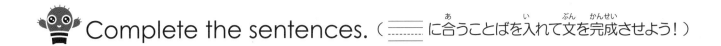 Complete the sentences. (＿＿ に合うことばを入れて文を完成させよう！)

① 彼は速く泳げます。

| | | | fast. |

② 私はお寿司が作れます。

| | | | sushi. |

③ あなたは英語を話せますか？

| | | | English? |

はい、話せます。

| | , | . |

④ 彼女はバスの運転ができますか？

| | | | a bus? |

いいえ、できません。

| | , | . |

過去形の復習をしよう

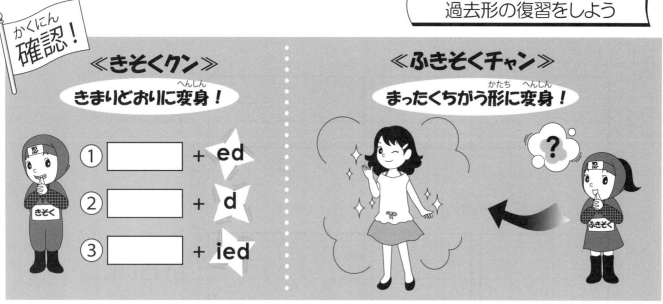

確認！

≪きそくクン≫
きまりどおりに変身！

① [   ] + **ed**
② [   ] + **d**
③ [   ] + **ied**

≪ふきそくチャン≫
まったくちがう形に変身！

Which group do the words belong to?
Write the correct group letter in the (   ).
（下の言葉は次のどっちのグループかな？ "**A**"か"**B**"を選んで（   ）に入れよう。）

≪きそくクングループ…**A**　ふきそくチャングループ…**B**≫

go　（   ）　　　cook （   ）

watch（   ）　　　eat　（   ）

have （   ）　　　help （   ）

open （   ）　　　close （   ）

see　（   ）　　　get　（   ）

live　（   ）　　　study （   ）

come（   ）　　　write （   ）

 Practice the past tense below. （ふきそくチャンの練習！）

(begin → began)

① began

(bring → brought)

② brought

(feel → felt)

③ felt

(find → found)

④ found

(forget → forgot)

⑤ forgot

(know → knew)

⑥ knew

(lose → lost)

⑦ lost

Practice the past tense below. （ふきそくチャンの練習！）

(meet → met)

① met

(say → said)

② said

(see → saw)

③ saw

(think → thought)

④ thought

(take → took)

⑤ took

(tell → told)

⑥ told

苦手な単語を練習しよう！

Practice the past tense below. （きそくクンの練習！）

(clean → cleaned)

① cleaned

(finish → finished)

② finished

(show → showed)

③ showed

(talk → talked)

④ talked

(wait → waited)

⑤ waited

Special Review

苦手な単語を練習しよう！

過去形の復習をしよう

≪きそくクン≫
きまりどおりに変身！

① ☐ + ed
② ☐ + d
③ ☐ + ied

≪ふきそくチャン≫
まったくちがう形に変身！

？

≪そのまんま丸≫
まったく変化なし！

変身はできないワン！

新登場！！

Practice the past tense below. （ふきそくチャンの練習！）

(意味)

(become → became)

① became

(break → broke)

② broke

(choose → chose)

③ chose

(fall → fell)

④ fell

(grow → grew)

⑤ grew

(意味)

(leave → left)

⑥ left

(drive → drove)

⑦ drove

(build → built)

⑧ built

Practice the past tense below. (きそくクンの練習!)

(意味)

(arrive → arrived)

① arrived

(call → called)

② called

(carry → carried)

③ carried

(count → counted)

④ counted

(decide → decided)

⑤ decided

(意味)

(enjoy → enjoyed)

⑥ enjoyed

(invite → invited)

⑦ invited

(visit → visited)

⑧ visited

変身は
できないワン!

新登場!!

Practice the past tense below. (そのまんま丸の練習)

(意味)

(hit → hit)

① hit

(hurt → hurt)

② hurt

Special Review

苦手な単語を練習しよう!

Find the letters that spell the past tense forms of the following verbs. Write them on the lines and then write the Japanese in the (   ).

（下の□から文字をさがして絵に合う言葉の過去形を＿＿＿＿の上に書き（　）には日本語を入れよう！）

① (fall) _____
(   )

② (hurt) _____
(   )

③ (grow) _____
(   )

④ (choose) _____
(   )

⑤ (leave) _____
(   )

⑥ (drive) _____
(   )

Circle the letters you use. （上で使った文字は ◯ でかこもう！）

```
f   e   f   u   r   e   d   c

h   t   v       b   h   w   e
        o

o   k   r   e   s   r   l

r   l   e   g   t   l   o   e
```

Use the remaining letters to spell the past tense form of one of the new verbs in this book.
Write the verb and then write the Japanese in the (   ).

（上に ◯ 印がつかなかった文字を使って過去形を1つ作り、（　）には日本語を書こう！）

_____
(   )

-149-